JOURNAL OF MULTI BUSINESS MODEL INNOVATION AND TECHNOLOGY

Volume 3, No. 3 (September 2015)

JOURNAL OF MULTI BUSINESS MODEL INNOVATION AND TECHNOLOGY

Aim of the journal
Provides an in-depth and holistic view of Multi Business Model and technology Innovation from practical to theoretical aspects covering topics that are equally valuable for practitioners as well as academia - also those new in the field.

Scope of the journal
The journal covers Multi Business Model and technology innovation issues and solutions thereof. As Business has moved towards a world of multi business models, issues in modeling business and business models will be published. The publication takes a holistic, strategical, network based and global view to the Multi business approach. Some example topics are: Multi Business Model Innovation and technology in Health Care sector, Multi Business Model Innovation Leadership and management in SME´s, Cloud based Multi Business Model Innovation, Business Model Eco systems, Open and Closed Business Models

Published, sold and distributed by:
River Publishers
Niels Jernes Vej 10
9220 Aalborg Ø
Denmark

River Publishers
Lange Geer 44
2611 PW Delft
The Netherlands

Tel.: +45369953197
www.riverpublishers.com

Journal of Multi Business Model Innovation and Technology is published three times a year. Publication programme, 2015: Volume 3 (3 issues)

ISSN 2245-456X
ISBN 978-87-93379-60-2

JOURNAL OF MULTI BUSINESS MODEL INNOVATION AND TECHNOLOGY

Volume 3, No. 3 September 2015

Introduction

This issue is the last issue of Volume 3, 2015. The thematic focus for all the issues in Volume 3 has been a contribution to the state of art within Scandinavian innovation and business model innovation research. In Volume 3, Issue 3, September 2015, focus are researchers representing M-BIT Research Group in Denmark (**M**ulti **B**usiness **I**nnovation and **T**echnology). M-BIT was founded in 2012 at Aalborg University by the authors of the Two Black Boxes article. In this introduction I quote and repeat from the article written by Ole Horn Rasmussen in this journals Volume 3, Issue 1 – "Industrial Business Model Innovation in Scandinavia – A Contribution to the State of the Art 2015", where I introduced M-BIT and the Two Black Boxes article.

"The research set-up (of M-BIT – my insertion), can be identified from this figure:

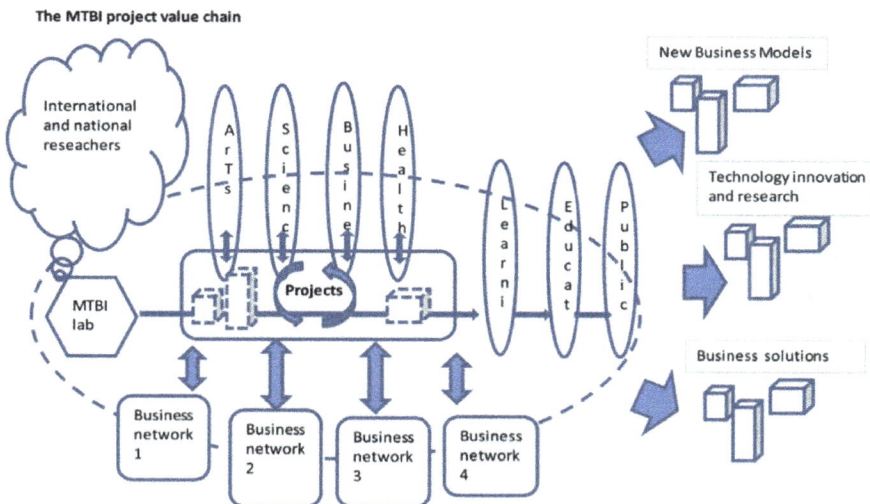

The MTBI project value chain

As the model indicates, M-BIT works close together with the industry. The industry is defined total broadly and includes any business – private, public, semi-private, voluntary organizations etc. Any unit is understood as a business and a business is understood as an organization with many units – or as M-BIT prefers to pronounce it: Business Models. During participatory actions research the aim is to contribute with both theoretical and practical results. It means that students, business managers, workers, academia, business organizations, public authorities gain from the groups work.

The article in Volume 3, Issue 3 is conceptual and aims to contribute to the ontological, epistemological and methodological discussion toward a theory of business model and business model innovation. In the Lakatos sense the paper aims to contribute to the establishment of a research program for business model innovation on the one side and on the other side the paper aims to support the practical BMI efforts to implement concrete BMI actions in the businesses. The paper contributes by qualifying with an answer to "Where must managers look in order to release the BMI potential of their business?"

The question may be an easy task. However, there is two black boxes – a business and the surrounding of the business – and the coherence between them. **The authors raise the fundamental question that the black boxes cannot be taken for granted. Consequently, they ask: What does theory tell about the black boxes and how to understand them?** Based upon a holistic approach they investigate if and how different approaches are able to work together. The foundation of the article is a combined top-down and down-up thinking, and establishes an overview that reflects the whole "battlefield" for a business. The article argues for the existence of three arch types of business models: a macro BM, a micro BM and a micro-micro BM. A main element and a methodological reflection has an initial reference to the general idea about Ecosystem and the idea of BM Ecosystems (BMES). A main point is that a concrete and practical focus on eco-systems also puts focus on the "unborn" business opportunities. The authors point of departure is a discussion of the usefulness of the idea of National Systems of Innovation and the usefulness of the idea about industry, clusters and sectors. The assumption is that the links between Business Model Components, Business Model Dimensions, Business Models, Business Model portfolio, the Business, Ecosystems and the different Business Model Eco-systems represent the potential for any BMI process, which together with some general rules of the game, as defined by Veblen, lay down the framework conditions for a business' BMI process. The paper concludes, that the idea of national systems of innovation must be supplemented with other perspectives. Because the idea of clusters, sectors and industries is rooted in the understanding of a business as the unit in focus, these ideas must be supplemented because any business consists of more than one BM. Within a multi business model focus the coherence and interplay between AS-IS BMs and TO-BE BMs represent a theoretical and practical necessity. Besides, it might be valuable to rethink the term barriers and borders to industry, sections and clusters and instead think as context based. The boarders of ecosystems depend on the context and the viewpoint.

The idea of a business-model as a cube works in practice. However, the paper presents two "Where to Look Models" evolved from a top-down and a down-top perspective – respectively. The Models "Where to Look" is about understanding the research field for a business. The models represent the real "Battle-field" or as we argue: The practical research field for the business in question. Any BM is unique. The consequence will be that every business will have its own, specific and context dependent research field or what we term: Business Model Eco-Systems".

Kind regards
Editor Ole Horn Rasmussen
Postdoc, Ph.D., Msc. Economics
Aarhus University, Denmark

Two Black Boxes: Understanding the Coherence between Business Models & Business Model Eco Systems – A Contribution toward a Definition of the Object for Business Model Innovation and the Question of "Where to Look"?

Ole Horn Rasmussen and Peter Lindgren

M-BIT Research Group, Aarhus University, Denmark
E-mail: ohr@auhe.au.dk; ohr@Btech.au.dk; ole.horn.rasmussen@gmail.com;
peterli@hih.au.dk

Received 16 June 2015; Accepted 15 September 2015;
Publication 10 March 2016

Quotation of Article

Horn Rasmussen, O, Lindgren, P (2016), Two Black Boxes: Understanding the Coherence between Business Models & Business Model Eco Systems – A Contribution toward a Definition of the Object for Business Model Innovation and the Question of "Where to Look"?

Abstract

This paper is conceptual and aims to contribute to the ontological, epistemological and methodological discussion toward a theory of business model and business model innovation. In the Lakatos sense the paper aims to contribute to the establishment of a research program for business model innovation on the one side and on the other side the paper aims to support the practical BMI efforts to implement concrete BMI actions in the businesses. The paper contributes by qualifying with an answer to "Where must managers look in

Journal of Multi Business Model Innovation and Technology, Vol. 3, 67–132.
doi: 10.13052/jmbmit2245-456X.331

order to release the BMI potential of their business?" during deepening the understanding of the two black boxes – a business and the surrounding of the business – and the coherence between them. We simply cannot take the two black boxes for given.

Trying to have a holistic approach we are forced to investigate if and how different approaches are able to work together. The paper builts on a top-down and down-up thinking, respectively, and establish an overview that reflects the whole "battlefield" for a business. A main element and the methodological reflection has an initial reference to the general idea about Ecosystem and the idea of BM Ecosystems (BMES), where point of departure is a discussion of the usefulness of the idea of National Systems of Innovation and the usefulness of the idea about industry, clusters and sectors within our context. The links between Business Model Components, Business Model Dimensions, Business Models, Business Model portfolio, the Business, Ecosystems and the different Business Model Eco-systems represent the potential for any BMI process, which together with some general rules of the game, as defined by Veblen, lay down the framework conditions for a business' BMI process. The relation-axiom of business models assists us in getting an overview. The paper concludes, that the idea of national systems of innovation must be supplemented with other perspectives. Because the idea of clusters, sectors and industries is rooted in the understanding of a business as the unit in focus, these ideas must be supplemented because any business consists of more than one BM. Within a multi business model focus the coherence and interplay between AS-IS BMs and TO BE BMs represent a theoretical and practical necessity. It might be valuable to rethink the term barriers and borders to industry, sections and clusters and instead think as context based. The boarders of ecosystems depend on the context and the viewpoint.

Experiences with BM construction point on the importance of focus on different sub-areas, the idea of co-option and the need to incorporate the idea of time. The idea of a global system of eco-systems seems to enrich the discussion of framework conditions for the BMI process. A main point is that a concrete and practical focus on eco-systems also puts focus on the "un-born" business opportunities. The idea of a business-model as a cube works in practice. However, the need to break down the business not only into different business models but to break down each business model into different dimensions and further into different components enriches the explanation and understanding of the actual releasing of the innovation potential in the BMI process. Finally, the Veblenian general theory – which put the evolutionary economic business process into an institutional and actor teleological context – contributes to enrich explanation and understanding of the economic process including the BMI process and "Where to look?" The paper presents two "Where to Look Models" evolved from a top-down and a down-top perspective – respectively. The Models "Where to Look" is about understanding the research field for a business. Both models have a theoretical and a heuristic purpose, where the Down-Top model represents the real "Battle-field" or as we argue: The practical research field for the business in question. Any BM is unique. The consequence will be that every business will have its own, specific and context dependent research field or what we term: Business Model Eco-Systems.

Design/Methodology/Approach

The paper provides a theoretical and conceptual study for different potential understandings of the object for BMI, where the approach is to let the different theoretical perspectives "talk for themselves" and then forward our theoretical framework within a discussion including different empiric illustrations. The answers is given from two distinct different perspectives. A pure economic theoretical perspective represented by the institutional, evolutionary and co-evolutionary economist Thorstein Veblen and a more cross-disciplinary and combined primarily macro- and micro- economically methodologically perspective. One methodological challenge in the research process is to test the usefulness of an Elster/Lawson combination. Elster's idea is to go from macro to micro, i.e. reductionism, while the philosophy of Tony Lawson points in the direction of the meta-universe. The methodological idea is that such a combination contributes to a framework or theory of business models and business model innovation.

The empiric research methodology is a participating action research approach.

Practical Implications

Businesses struggle continuously with releasing more value from their business BM's. This challenge exists because of the economic organization and the inherent conservative institutions. Accepting our framework introduces a need for a discussion of new strategies at both a micro- and macroeconomic level in order to improve and increase the release of a business' BM potential within the process of BMI. The outcomes of the paper is a first contribution and overview of different business BM's relations to other BM eco-systems and a creation and contribution to understand the general framework conditions related to releasing business' BMs potential in the economic system.

Keywords: Innovation, Eco-Systems, Business Model Eco-Systems, Empirical Object, Methodology, Framework Conditions for Business Model Innovation, Economic Theory, Business Theory, Business Management, Business Model Theory Construction, Lakatos.

1 Introduction

The overall aim with the paper is to contribute to a new research program in the Lakatos sense with focus on business models and business model innovation (Lecocq, Demil & Ventura 2010). The title of the paper: – Two Black Boxes: Understanding the Coherence between Business models & Business Model Eco systems – A Contribution toward a definition of the object for Business Model Innovation and the question of "Where to Look"? – indicates that we as a point of departure see the idea of Business Models and the idea of Business Model Eco Systems as black boxes. What are there in the boxes? This paper aims to contribute to answer the question from two distinct different perspectives. A pure economic theoretical perspective represented by the institutional, evolutionary and co-evolutionary economist Thorstein Veblen and a more cross-disciplinary and combined primarily macro- and microeconomically methodologically perspective. Both perspectives address the object for business model innovation and tend to contribute to an understanding of where a business dealing with innovation activities must look. Another way to express the aim of the paper is the idea that when a business intend to practice Business Model Innovation it is crucial for the management of the business to know and have an overview according to both the general and the "business-specific" framework conditions for the Business Model Innovation process of the business model in question. "Where to look" represent in this context the framework conditions taken as a whole.

From a system – or macro – point of view – the idea of business model innovation and the releasing of its BM innovation potential gets into a huge dilemma if the theoretical works of Thorstein Veblen acts as one of the cornerstones in order to understand Business Model Eco-systems. Per definition the process meets a systemic framework where the normative idea of rationality becomes part of the theoretical and practical discussion with reference to at least three themes. First of all we have what Veblen announces as "The State of Industrial Art". It refers to the mish-match between what the economy is able to produce compared with what the economy in practice produce. Secondly, and this is the main focus in this paper, the theoretical work of Veblen operates with a cavalry of actors. Each actor is bound up into a specific intentional acting defined at a general level. Because the Veblenian approach is highly abstract there is a need for qualified definition of the empirical object for Business Model Innovation (BMI). Our contribution to this task and the methodological reflection has an initial reference to the idea of Eco-Systems and the idea of BM Ecosystems (BMES), where our point of departure is a discussion of the usefulness of the idea of National Systems of Innovation and the usefulness of the idea about industry, clusters and sectors within our context.

There is until now no accepted language for Ecosystems. Consequently, the contribution from the paper is explorative. The paper attempt to contribute by proposing how the links between Business Model Components, Business Model Dimensions, Business Models (The Cubes), Business Model portfolio, the Business, Ecosystems and the different Business Model Ecosystems represent the potential for any BMI process, which together with some general rules of the game, as defined by Veblen, lay down the framework conditions for a business' BMI process. The paper is primarily theoretical but it is rooted in and evolved in close connection with practice and our experience form working together with different businesses[1] for many years during participative action research methodology.

2 The Paper and the Idea of Ontology, Epistemology and Methodology

The paper is conceptual and has an explicit reference to the idea of ontology, epistemology and methodology. The main purpose is to contribute to the evolution of a framework and theory of business models and business model innovation (Lecocq, Demil & Ventura 2010). General speaking the paper is just one contribution and the paper must be seen as part of a whole. The methodological reflection has reference to ontology[2] and the idea of explanation. The most influential theoreticians are Roy Bhaskar and Tony Lawson (Lawson 2003a, Lawson 2003b, Lawson 1997) and Jon Elster (Elster 1983: ; Elster 1986: ; Elster 1989). The reflections of Lawson, based upon

---

[1]Talking about business the term covers any kind of business – public institutions, private institutions, mixed public/private institutions etc. In the practical work the crucial question is the delimination of the unit in question – not whether it is public or private. As a matter of definition the unit which is in focus must be understood as an independent unit (even the unit is part of e.g. a larger business/institution). This condition is crucial for how to arrange and implement the concrete BMI process.

[2]"By ontology I mean the study (or theory) of being or existence, a concern with the nature and structure of the "stuff" of reality. Now, all methods have ontological presuppositions or preconditions, that is conditions under which their usage is appropriate" (Lawson 2003b, page 12).

the thoughts developed by Bhaskar, belong to critical realism. They aspire to develop a universal ontology of economics. On the one hand, this ambition can be postulated to represent an alternative means of thinking as compared with Elster and the discussion in which the potential of multiple explanations is offered[3]. On the other hand, Lawson and Bhaskar argue for the existence of an ontological hierarchy of explanations within economics. Their method is to seek behind the cause to the cause of the cause etc. This implies a position of endless regress. We can never be absolutely certain that we have found the truth. This also indicates a kind of openness to multiple explanations. One methodological challenge in the research process is to test the usefulness of an Elster/Lawson combination. Elster's idea is to go from macro to micro, i.e. reductionism. He focuses on explanation by mechanisms.

> To explain is to provide a mechanism, to open up the black box and show how the nuts and bolts, the cogs and wheels of the internal machinery (Here the term "mechanism" should be understood broadly, to cover intentional chains from a goal to an action as well as causal chains from an event to its effects) (Elster 1983, page 24).

Our task is broader,. We are inspired by the term "transformation". Transformation is a result of a radical change in at least one of the central rules of the game (Horn Rasmussen 2008). A demarcation to a focus on mechanisms would make the term "mechanisms" identical with the term "rules of the game". This is not our initial intention. While Elster's universe is the micro-foundation of the economy and a general neglect of anything other than the micro-universe, the philosophy of Tony Lawson as based upon Bhaskar points in the direction of the meta-universe. Methodologically, the combination between Elster and his priority on causal and intentional explanations within social science, and the search for an universal meta ontology as inspired by Lawson is on the one hand contra-dictionary. On the other hand, the methodological idea is that such a combination may involve more theoretical insights. This may contribute with a heuristic element to the research process toward contribution to a framework or theory of the idea of business models and business model innovation. The latter argument supports the attempt to make such methodological combination.

This leads us to a position where a construction a kind of patchwork of explanations may contribute insight to our research. However, as we are

---

[3]In Elster (Elster 1983) the idea of explanations (causal, functional and intentional explanations) is confronted with theories of technical change (neoclassical theories, Schumpeter's theory, evolutionary theories and marxist theories).

going to demonstrate much of the patchwork construction may very well refer to the theoretical perspective. What level of abstraction does the arguments belong to? The task may be implemented as adequately as possibly. As one might already notice, this brings us to the first consequence of our study; when we conclude, we have merely made a contribution to a new beginning based upon a deeper understanding. This is the position of the critical realism approach, which by definition always will argue in such a manner. Besides, there is a link to Lakatos (Latsis 1976) and his epistemological and methodological approach for a continuously search for and establishment of a new research program. By now, the link between explanations and understanding should be indicated. Understanding represents the deepest archive of knowledge. Explanations are the means, while understanding is the aim. The general issue in this methodological reflection concerning what could be perceived as "A contribution to a concept of explanations in order to reach a better understanding." The task is not to neglect a search for a model, but rather, the ambition *to create an initial foundation for a model or in our context a theoretical model with reference to business models and business model innovation during the compilation of different theories.*

This forwards a crucial question; how do we select our theoretical elements? What are the arguments and what is our delimitation? First of all we take our theoretical point of departure at a macro economic level. The Economics of Thorstein Veblen is from our perspective interesting. Among other crucial theoretical elements he argues for certain systemic limitation for any BMI process. The Veblenian perspective offers important insights in order to understand the question of systemic limitations in the process of BMI or as some argues – Business model construction (Heikkilä, Kuivaniemi 2012). It is uncontroversial to postulate that the object for any BMI process is defined by whatever exist of material and immaterial elements and whatever that is on its way to exist. How can we contribute to qualify to an understanding of the object for BMI? Within a macro level the idea of National System of Innovation has for a long academic period contributed to define the foundation of the knowledge economy. Within business economics the idea of clusters, industry and sections have a dominant platform. However, recently the idea of eco-systems have been much debated both within the academic and industrial communities. Based upon this compilation we are going to present a contribution to how to create a link between a macro and a micro perspective with an explicit reference to business models (BM), business model innovation (BMI), Eco-Systems (ES) and Business Model Eco-Systems (BMES).

3 Research Question

For managers of business our research indicates that the unawareness of understanding their own business models and the surroundings of the BMs lead to an unreleased potential related to BMI. The basic for a business is firstly to know and define their own "AS – IS" BMs. Next step is to know af define the surroundings. Then the business can start "seeing" BMs and BMs relations to the surroundings from different perspectives. Last step is making different scenarios in the business related to the surroundings in order to choose the strategic direction for the different BMs in the business. This paper addresses none of the above steps but focus on the foundation for taking the steps. Before a business is able to implement a well qualified work for "How to Look?" it is important for a business to know "Where to look?". Consequently, the general research question is: Where must managers look in order to release the BMI potential of their business? The hypothesis is that it is a question of understanding two black boxes – a business and the surrounding of the business (see Figure 1) – and the coherence between them. **We simply cannot take the two black boxes for given.**

The research question will be answered from two very different points of abstraction, where the connection is their contribution to understand the general framework conditions for any BMI process. As outlined in the previous section, the idea is that a combination of different explanations and understandings – within different levels of abstraction – will increase

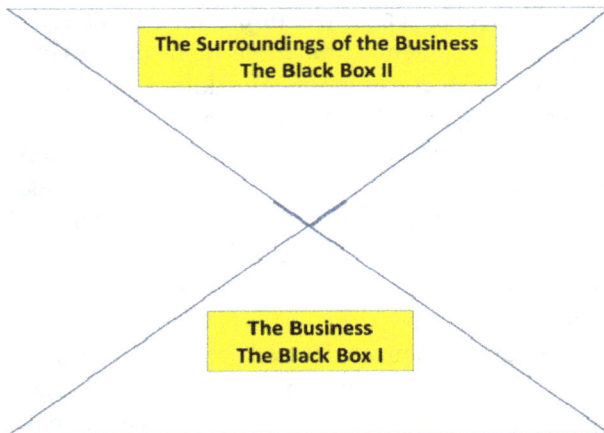

Figure 1   Two Black Boxes – What is inside – Definitions?

Source: (Horn Rasmussen, Lindgren & Saghaug 2014).

our general archive of knowledge and contribute to improve the theoretical knowledge in the academic communities with reference to the object of the business model innovation processes. Such potential for increasing the existing knowledge has practical importance for the concrete BMI work within the businesses at a micro economic level and is a first step towards doing BMI strategically.

4 Black Box I and II Seen from an Abstract Theoretical Perspective: The State of Industrial Art – Veblen and His Contribution to Understand Business Models, Business Model Innovation, Eco-Systems and IC

It is our hypothesis that The General Theory of Veblen as outlined by (Horn Rasmussen 2008) may contribute to the understanding of Business Models, Business Model Innovation, Eco-Systems and a general limitation for the economic process. The theoretical work of Veblen is complex. Point of departure is the seven elements in The General Theory and we show how some of them can be linked to both the theoretical and empirical work related to BM, BMI and Eco-Systems.

The elements are:

1. The Mechanism: The Interstitial Adjustment of the Industrial System[4]
2. The Mechanism: All politics are business – Politics one
3. The Institution: Make Believe
4. The Institution: State of Industrial Art
5. The Institution: Politics two
6. Evolution of the Actor Cavalry
7. Evolution from handicraft to modern system 1 and 2

Focus in this paper is the institution "State of the Industrial Art" and "The evolution of the Actor Cavalry". The "State of the Industrial Art" in the Veblenian understanding is a logical result of the economic organization in – what has been named Modern State II or the second era of capitalism (Horn Rasmussen 2008). The institution represents a central framework condition where the macro perspective is transformed into the practical framework conditions at a business or a micro economic level and have address to the ability to release in the BMI process. *From a Veblenian point of view and within our context, "The state of industrial art" can be defined as the result*

---

[4]Because the term is rather unknown we present the definition in appendix I.

of the interaction of the two black boxes. We can also characterize "The State of Industrial art" as an abstract global eco-system and a general framework condition for releasing the potential in the BMI process. The state of industrial art is the institution that science and technology are able to produce more goods and services than are actually implemented in society. This indicates the immaterial dimension of the institution. On the other hand, the technology and knowledge actually exists, which indicates the material dimension of the institution. It is a matter of *the rate of exploitation of the technology and knowledge.* By this consideration, the existence of an inherent mismatch between "actual and potential use of the industrial state of art" is established. Here the evolution of the actor cavalry is central, which also has changed from modern state I to modern state II. In Modern State II industry and businessmen became separated and new rules of the game entered the economic process including the BMI processes. Veblen's intention is to demonstrate an inherent opposition between businessmen, on the one side, and "the outcome of the work of those men who are engaged in the industrial employment", on the other side. The latter consists of the "inventors, engineers, experts, or whatever name be applied to the comprehensive class that does the intellectual work involved in the modern machine industry" (Veblen 1978, (1904 page 19–20)). We must recall that their position in the actor-cavalry – which is his definition the actors in the economic system – is as workers or the common man. However, these wage-earning intellectuals pave the way for the businessmen. Taken together we suggest that at a global and general level of abstraction "The State of Industrial Art" can be compared with the overall object for BMI – The Global Eco-system and the economic process at both a microeconomic and a macroeconomic level". From a Veblenian position the idea of "stock and flow" is overlapping (Horn Rasmussen 2008) and consequently the institution "The State of Industrial Art" consists of both a dynamic and a static dimension. As a matter of definition: Within a Veblenian perspective "The eco-system represents a potential which is unused". This interpretation of the economic macro-system is straight in line with the framework we argue is reality within a business model perspective (Lindgren, Horn Rasmussen 2013, Horn Rasmussen, Lindgren & Saghaug 2014). Consequently, our theoretical and empirical perspective and the Veblenian approach reach the same framework conditions – however from two different viewpoints. And within two different concepts of reasons.

Proceeding further with Veblen and his treatment of innovation, he states that modern technology has roots in workmanship. "The live-stock expert is soberly learning by trial and error what to attempt and how to go about it in his breeding experiments, and he deals as callously as any mechanical engineer with the chemistry of stock foods and the use and abuse of ferments, germs and enzymes" (Veblen 1914, 1964 page 198). While this was the typical situation in the HT-era, technological development in the modern era, starting in M1 and further intensified in M2, used science to accelerate the technological opportunities. An effect of the machine process was further demand for education and increased knowledge. This has been a cumulative process.

> And here and now, as always and everywhere, invention is the mother of necessity ... Any such innovation that fits workably ... will presently make its way into general and imperative use ... Any technological advantage gained by one competitor forthwith becomes a necessity to all the rest, on pain of defeat (Veblen 1914, 1964 page 314–315).

This is Veblen's position with respect to innovation, technological advance and the competitive system and Horn Rasmussen (Horn Rasmussen 2008) remarks that Veblen was ahead the idea about "the treadmill and cannibalism" official outlined by Cochrane in 1958 with theoretical reference to Schumpeter. The special position of the close relations between technology and science is crucial. "At no earlier period has the correlation between science and technology been so close ... the relation between current technology and the science is a relation of mutual give and take" (Veblen 1914, 1964 page 322–323). The empiric relevance of the Veblenian approach is illustrated in a conference paper (Horn Rasmussen, Lindgren & Saghaug 2014). However, a very brief illustration can be taken from the investment "Better Place" – this case is quoted from Wikipedia May, 2015.

Better Place was a venture-backed international business model[5] that developed and sold battery-charging and battery-switching services for electric cars. It was formally based in Palo Alto, California, but the bulk of its planning and operations were steered from Israel, where both its founder Shai Agassi and its chief investors resided. The business model opened its first functional charging station the first week of December 2008 at Cinema City

---

[5]We have replaced the term "Company" in the quote from Wikipedia concerning Better Place from a heuristic perspective. It is important to underline that this is a case seen from a business-level abstraction point of view, and not from a business model level abstraction point of view according to our theoretical understanding. We will proceed with this later on in the paper.

in Pi-Glilot near Tel Aviv, Israel. The first customer deliveries of Renault Fluence Z.E. electric cars enabled with battery switching technology began in Israel in the second quarter of 2012, and at peak in mid September 2012, there were 21 operational battery-swap stations open to the public in Israel. ...... The high investment required to develop the charging and swapping infrastructure, and a market penetration far lower than originally predicted by Shai Agassi. Less than 1,000 Fluence Z.E. cars were deployed in Israel and around 400 units in Denmark, after spending about US$850 million in private capital. After two failed post-bankruptcy acquisition attempts, the bankruptcy receivers sold off the remaining assets in November 2013 to Grngy for only $450,000.

Having the framework from Veblen, it is an obviously empirical indication that the strength of what Veblen calls "The Captain of Industry" clearly was underestimated by the investors, who failed in their ability to implement their electric car concept. However, the evolution of the market for electric cars in e.g. Norway indicates that politics can create transformation due change in "the existing rules of the game" (Grønkjær 2015). While there in Denmark April 2015 are 3.745 electric cars number 50.000 was reached in Norway, April 2015. The illustration indicates that the question of "Where to look?" when a business implement BMI can be qualified by involving a pure theoretical thinking and transfer the theoretical thinking into an empiric business case or object.

5 Black Box I and II Seen from a more Concrete Perspective: The idea of Industry, Sections, Clusters, National System of Innovation and Eco-systems

While the Veblenian approach and connection to BM and BMI is characterized as a macro-approach at a high level of abstraction, we need to discuss how this approach can be linked to a more concrete macro and micro object. We find that the idea of industry (clusters), sections, national systems of innovation and eco-systems contribute to a further understanding of the object for BMI and consequently the question about the framework conditions for releasing a given and context dependent BMI potential.

5.1 National Systems of Innovation and BMI

In order to qualify the discussion we – as an exercise – go back to "a kind of zero". It is uncontroversial to claim that a business can be defined as part of its surroundings. We illustrated this statement in Figure 1 with the idea of the existence of two black boxes.

The figure indicates som kind of coherence between the black boxes and we find that it is uncontroversial to argue that the process of BMI involves an interaction between the business and the surroundings of the business.

The main question is where to look when the ambition is to link A and B – the Black Box I and the Black Box II?

Much of the ideas about innovation and how innovation activity is suited best could start with the idea of understanding a national system of innovation (e.g. (Nelson 1993, Freeman 1995, Lundvall 2010). Because, on a global scale, it is also uncontroversial to argue that in such case the surroundings or "The Black Box II" can be defined as the sum of nations, states etc. or in general the surroundings can be defined as the surroundings defined at a global scale. Then we have another model as shown in Figure 2.

We must discuss the idea of the illustration in Figure 2. First – and this may be controversial. Can we include e.g. customers, network partners and competitors to a certain business – which obviously must be defined as an important part to a business – as being an automatically part of a certain

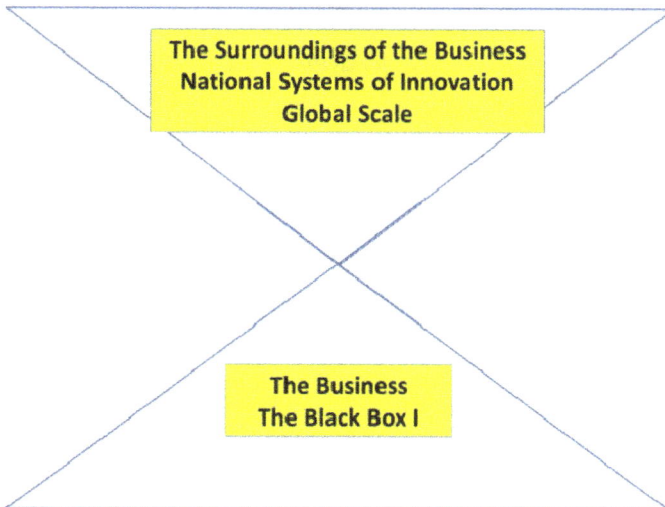

Figure 2   Black Box 2 defined by National systems of Innovation at a Global Scale.

Source: (Horn Rasmussen, Lindgren & Saghaug 2014).

national system of innovation? According to Wikipedia "National System of Innovation can be defined as the flow of technology and information among people, enterprises and institutions which is key to the innovative process on the national level. According to innovation system theory, innovation and technology development are results of a complex set of relationships among actors in the system, which includes enterprises, universities and government research institutes. The Term originated when Christopher Freemann and Bengt-Åke Lundvall worked together in the late 1980s. Freeman's research drew heavily on political economy of Friedrich List and historical account of the rise of Japan as an economic superpower. Lundvall's work explored the important social interactions between suppliers and customers and their role in encouraging innovation in Denmark. Apart from a general definition, as above, there is no canonical definition of national innovation systems. A few dominant definitions are listed below (quoted by the OECD publication national Innovation Systems 1997) which overlap quite a bit:

A national system of innovation has e.g. been defined as follows:

- ... *the network of institutions in the public and private sectors whose activities and interactions initiate, import, modify and diffuse new technologies.* Freeman, C. (1995), "The National System of Innovation in Historical Perspective", Cambridge Journal of Economics, No. 19, pp. 5–24
- ... *the elements and relationships which interact in the production, diffusion and use of new, and economically useful, knowledge ... and are either located within or rooted inside the borders of a nation state.* Lundvall, B-Å. (ed.) (1992). National Innovation Systems: Towards a Theory of Innovation and Interactive Learning, Pinter, London.
- ... *a set of institutions whose interactions determine the innovative performance ... of national firms.* Nelson, R. (ed.) (1993), National Innovation Systems. A Comparative Analysis, Oxford University Press, New York/Oxford". http://en.wikipedia.org/wiki/National_System_of_ Innovation (March, 2013).

What is important for us is not the precisely definition even the idea of definitions belongs to the core within social science. As the different definitions indicate there exist research communities who focus on the link between a nation and its innovative activities. One solution could be to define the Black Box II as National Systems of Innovation as indicated above. From a practical point of view the acknowledgement of the existence of national systems of innovation means that much efforts have been implemented among different stakeholders like governments, ministries, regional authorities, research communities and consultants on a global scale in order to describe the systems and bring forward policy proposals and implement politics. With an increasing tendency during the last decades the area of innovation has been object to much attention. However, much attention among stakeholders has been with point of departure in a macro perspective and consequently such activity has influenced the dimension of politi – or in a practical language the framework conditions for innovation activities.

What happens if we claim that the idea and focus on a national innovation system represents an old-fashion way of thinking?

We assume, that we need to include a more modern notion of eco-systems and sub-ecosystems into the idea of where the potential for innovation exist. Besides, because of our theoretical and practical assumptions that the root to successful and strategic innovation must be based upon the existing raw materials with special attention on relations in the business a specific understanding of the business must also be incorporated in our way of thinking (Horn Rasmussen, Lindgren & Saghaug 2014). The mission is – as mentioned in the ontology section, to expand the idea of the framework conditions and take an exclusive focus on a bottom-up perspective as a supplement to the top-down macro-perspective. In this paper the top-down point of view is represented on the one hand and on a highly level of theoretical abstraction by the Veblenian approach and on the other hand the idea of National system of innovation and the idea of eco-systems. In the first outlining we will abstract from Veblen and concentrate on the above referred definitions of a national system of innovation. We ask ourselves which definition might work well at both a macro and a micro level? It seems quite reasonable that the Lundvall-definition works well at both levels: *"the elements and relationships which interact in the production, diffusion and use of new, and economically useful, knowledge ... and are either located within or rooted inside the borders of a nation state"*. Exactly his focus on elements and relations that interact in the process of production is vital. However, as we latter on will present, the question about use of only new knowledge is rather questionable linked to our proposed framework for Business Model Innovation. Our point of departure is the existing knowledge as the fundamental basis for any business model innovation process. Taking a further critical point the explicit focus on technology and new technology seems a bit to narrow related to our understanding. Technology and new technology is only one, however important, part of our business model innovation framework. If we go further

---

Box 8: How to Study National Systems?

Our interest in utilizing the innovation system perspective is not purely academic. We use this concept as a focusing device in order to better understand how innovation affects economic development at the national level. Within this broad view many factors contribute to innovation and it might be seen as a problem that almost all aspects of society need to be brought in to explain the actual pattern of innovation. To structure the analysis it is useful to distinguish between the *core* of the innovation system and *the wider setting*. Both need to be included in the analysis since the aim is to link innovation to economic development.

Firms and the knowledge infrastructure constitute the core of the system. In principle we include all firms in the core since every firm has a potential for developing, absorbing or using new technology.

The wider setting refers to institutions that contribute to competence building and institutions that shape human interaction in relation to innovation. These include, first, family pattern, education system, career patterns in labour markets, inequality and social welfare systems. Second, they include the historical record of macroeconomic stability and the access to finance. Third, they include the final demand from households and public sector organizations. Fourth, they include government and public policy directly aiming at stimulating innovation, including diffusion and efficient use.

This way of setting the scene indicates a marginal role for public policy. What is intended is rather to see public policy mainly as intervening in relation to the core and the wider setting of the national innovation system. Alternatively we could see public policy as endogenous. To some degree we take this perspective in Edquist and Lundvall (1993) where we demonstrate how innovation policy in Sweden and Denmark tends to reproduce rather than renew the strengths of the respective system.

(Lundvall 2010, page 338).

into the ideas from Lundvall and his related research communities, we see how they find the research methodology should be dealing with studies around national innovation systems.

The research field within the Lundvall innovation paradigm operates with the core including all businesses. Besides, there are the widers settings defined by 4 categories. The definition seems as if anything matters. When we recall our methodological point of departure: Our postulate and consequently also our theoretical hypothesis is that we firstly is able to understand a business model, business model innovation and modelling its business model innovation strategy when we also consider the business models related to its out-out relations (Lindgren, Horn Rasmussen 2013)[6].

We briefly introduce our relation axiom. The relation axiom is the idea that Business Models can mapped within four different squares. In Figure 3, the situation is shown for the in-out square and in the example the BM is connected to two other BMs. Within a Lundvall perspective these models are implicit incorporated in his framework.

However, What about the out-out quadrant?[7] The model in Figure 4 illustrates the situation.

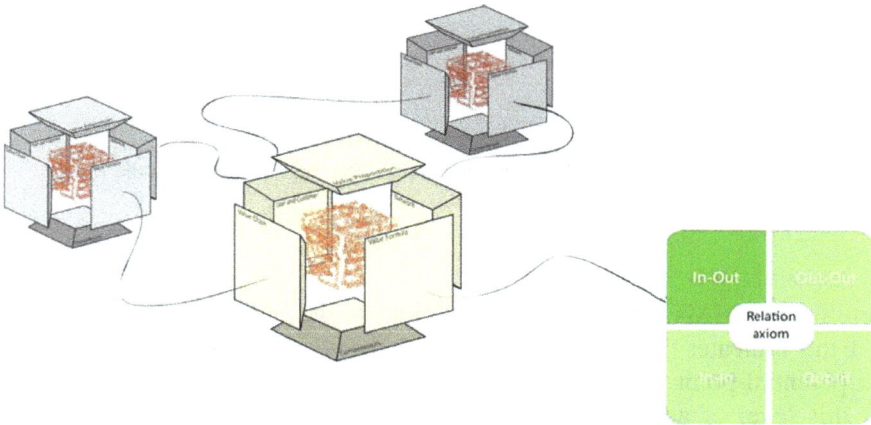

Figure 3 Relations from a BM inside the business to two other BMs in the surroundings.
Source: Inspired by (Lindgren, Horn Rasmussen 2013).

---

[6]The BM Cube will be further introduced later in the article.

[7]The last two quadrants in the relation axiom represents different situations. The Inside-In quadrant is where the business model looks into itself e.g. at dimensions level or component level. The outside-in quadrant is where focus is on the relations from BMs outside the BM in focus. Taken as a whole the four quadrants aims to create a holistic view upon a business and its business models.

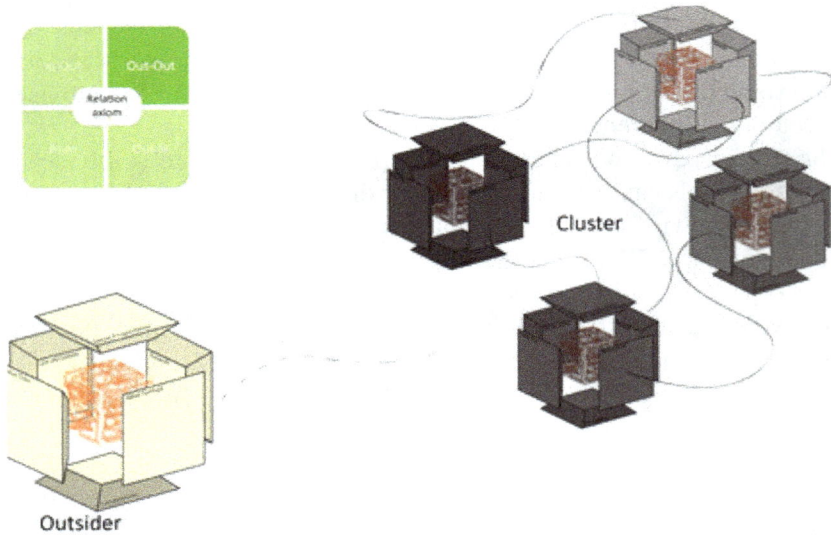

Figure 4   The Out-Out Quadrant of the Relation Axiom – Non relations between the BM in the Business and the BMs in the Out-Out Quadrant.

Source: Inspired by (Lindgren, Horn Rasmussen 2013).

Here focus is BMs which have non relations to the BMs of the business. By such this indicates that we also operate with the idea that anything matters from a potential point of view. Out-out relations are within our framework and at this level of abstraction relations between elements which doesn't have – at least at a first glance – connections to a business model in the business in question. Exactly the out-out relations are important in real life business model innovation activities. It is not the same as to argue that the slipstream from a butterfly (the relation between the elements: a butterfly and the atmosphere) in South-America affects a business model in Scandinavia. However, theoretically we simply can't neglect a possibly relation between the out-out relation and the business model. Having a global reference it is our claim that the surroundings to a business from a potential point of view can be defined as the national systems of innovation at a global scale. We know that this position challenge a scientific necessity with reference to building up demarcations, but we are going to demonstrate, that a demarcation a this step would ruin the idea of coming into the core of a more precisely understanding of Business Model Innovation and consequently the practical work of implementation of BMI-strategies[8]. Theoretically we work with an assumption, which belongs to our theoretical hard core in the Lakatos sense.

Our main point by making an explicit reference to the idea of a national innovation system is that we, bridge to our concept of a business and our concept of the Business-Model Relation Axiom. And even more specific: We qualify the idea of our Out-Out quadrant or square. If a business experiences that much of the national system of innovation is placed in the Out-Out quadrant, the business may have a problem concerning their innovation activity. And surely, if many businesses in a nation experience the same, there is a clear indicator that the national system of innovation doesn't fit to the businesses in the nation. Then the nation has a clear mish-match and consequently a clear problem. One may argue that we at these points are very speculative. However, the chains of arguments represent some explicit assumptions, which is part of the theoretical framework of our contributions toward a theory of business models, business model innovation and business model eco-systems.

5.2 Black Box II – Seen as Industry, Clusters or Sections versus the Eco-system Approach

We will briefly comment on the use of the terms industry, cluster and section because these terms could be argued to represent a well defined area in order to understand the object for BMI – Where to Look" – and consequently their potential reference to the Black Box II.

Many have tried to define a group of businesses as a cluster. In his Harvard Business Review article Porter (Porter 1998) has the following position which we under the headline: What is a Cluster?:

"What Is a Cluster?"

Clusters are geographic concentrations of interconnected companies and institutions in a particular field. Clusters encompass an array of linked industries and other entities important to competition. They include, for example, suppliers of specialized inputs such as components, machinery,

---

[8]Remark that we use plural dealing with the notion of strategy. The reason is a logically consequence of the assumption that a business always has more than one business model and it should be rather rare that all the BMs in the business follow and implement the same strategy. We assume that there must be implemented different strategies in a business where each BM follows it own strategy.

and services, and providers of specialized infrastructure. Clusters also often extend downstream to channels and customers and laterally to manufacturers of complementary products and to companies in industries related by skills, technologies, or common inputs. Finally, many clusters include governmental and other institutions—such as universities, standards-setting agencies, think tanks, vocational training providers, and trade associations—that provide specialized training, education, information, research, and technical support.

A cluster's boundaries are defined by the linkages and complementarities across industries and institutions that are most important to competition. Although clusters often fit within political boundaries, they may cross state or even national borders.

Clusters rarely conform to standard industrial classification systems, which fail to capture many important actors and relationships in competition. Thus significant clusters may be obscured or even go unrecognized. In Massachusetts, for example, more than 400 companies, representing at least 39,000 high-paying jobs, are involved in medical devices in some way. The cluster long remained all but invisible, however, buried within larger and overlapping industry categories such as electronic equipment and plastic products. Executives in the medical devices cluster have only recently come together to work on issues that will benefit them all.

Clusters promote both competition and cooperation. Rivals compete intensely to win and retain customers. Without vigorous competition, a cluster will fail. Yet there is also cooperation, much of it vertical, involving companies in related industries and local institutions. Competition can coexist with cooperation because they occur on different dimensions and among different players.

Clusters represent a kind of new spatial organizational form in between arm's-length markets on the one hand and hierarchies, or vertical integration, on the other. A cluster, then, is an alternative way of organizing the value chain. Compared with market transactions among dispersed and random buyers and sellers, the proximity of companies and institutions in one location—and the repeated exchanges among them—fosters better coordination and trust. Thus clusters mitigate the problems inherent in arm's-length relationships without imposing the inflexibilities of vertical integration or the management challenges of creating and maintaining formal linkages such as networks, alliances, and partnerships. A cluster of independent and informally linked companies and institutions represents a robust organizational form that offers advantages in efficiency, effectiveness, and flexibility."

A key element dealing with clusters is the question about having competitive advantages compared with other spaces – even at a global scale.

How about sector and industry? In the Industry Handbook Lanager (Langager 2015) comments on the difference. We quote Chad Langager:

"What is the difference between an industry and a sector?" By Chad Langager

The terms industry and sector are often used interchangeably to describe a group of companies that operate in the same segment of the economy or share a similar business type. Although the terms are commonly used interchangeably, they do, in fact, have slightly different meanings. This difference pertains to their scope; a sector refers to a large segment of the economy, while the term industry describes a much more specific group of companies or businesses.

A sector is one of a few general segments in the economy within which a large group of companies can be categorized. An economy can be broken down into about a dozen sectors, which can describe nearly all of the business activity in that economy. For example, the basic materials sector is the segment of the economy in which companies deal in the business of exploration, processing and selling the basic materials such as gold, silver or aluminum which are used by other sectors of the economy.

An industry, on the other hand, describes a much more specific grouping of companies with highly similar business activities. Essentially, industries are created by further breaking down sectors into more defined groupings. Each of the dozen or so sectors will have a varying number of industries, but it can be in the hundreds. For example, the financial sector can be broken down into industries such as asset management, life insurance and Northwest regional banks. The Northwest regional bank industry, which is part of the financial sector, will only contain companies that operate banks in the Northwestern states.

When breaking down the economy, the first groups are sectors which describe a general economic activity. Then all of the companies that fall into that sector are categorized further into industries where they are grouped only with companies with which they share very similar business activities. This is not the end, however. Industries can be further sub-categorized into various, more specific groupings.

It should be noted that you may find situations in which these two terms are reversed. However, the general idea remains: one breaks the economy down into a few general segments while the other further categorizes those into more specific business activities. In the stock market the generally accepted terminology cites a sector as a broad classification and an industry as a more specific one." (Langager 2015). http://www.investopedia.com/ask/answers/05/industrysector.asp

Porter (Porter 1985) defined an industry as referred

"to the environment and the forces close to a business that affect its ability to offer its value propositions to customers and make a profit"

Porter argued that a change in any of 5 forces – buyers, suppliers, new entrants, substitutes and exit and entry barriers normally would require that a business has to re-assess "the marketplace" given the overall change in industry formation.

The Industry could in this sense be regarded as equivalent to a BMES – however still taken into account that Porter argues to business operating in an industry and not businesses operating with one or more business models (Casadesus-Masanell, Ricart 2010, Lindgren, Horn Rasmussen 2013). Hereby – according to our findings – Porter may be lacking more or less some fundamental dimensions of a BMES. Further most cluster, sector and industry frameworks come out of a geographical and physical "thought world" (Dougherty 1992). Porter argued that cluster and industries help productivity, boost innovation and encourage new businesses to evolve. Porter also claimed that business' geographical proximity, their close competition with each other and the growth of specialized suppliers and production networks around them made a winning combination.

However many clusters and industries globally seems to be ailing e.g. because of they are victims of low-cost competition or in biological ecosystems they are "squeezed" out of their ecosystems by "smarter" species that have adapted to change in the fundamental conditions to the ecosystem, have a different want, need and demand to the output of the ecosystem – and "plays" a "different model" for survival and growth. Business today seems not to be able to protect themselves and hide behind the boarders – or barriers of a cluster, a sector or an industry as Porter proposed previously (Porter 1985). More open trade, improved transport links and the internet among other explanations mean that bunching together in a cluster, sector or an industry no longer offers strong defense against e.g. cheaper foreign rivals.

Fragmentation of production, value chains and outsourcing abroad are clear signs that business have become less competitive, weaken the networks on which clusters were built and may even facing that they are being destroyed their previous competitive advantage by clustering or acting as if clustering, sectors and industries still exists.

Porter introduced the terminology barriers related to Industries. In a BMES context we propose to increase this terminology as not just defined as related to physical and geographical barriers surrounding the BMES – but also related to the digital, virtual and maybe more important the perceptual barriers of the business. We propose that barriers in a BMES are context based and really dependent on "who are seeing and sensing" the barriers – or "boarders" of the BMES. A BMES formation – we propose – can be much wider than Porters Industry and Cluster term – and even cross or mix previous traditional defined cluster and industry barriers. We claim that this can be an explanation to why clusters and industries are suffering today – and even some vanishing – because they try to protect themselves behind barriers that really no longer exits – except in their or others (government, societies or even academics) perceptual picture and mental mindset.

The threat of substitute products and services, the threat of established rivals, and the threat of new entrants – **the 3 forces of horizontal competition** – and the bargaining power of suppliers and the bargaining power of customers – **the two forces from 'vertical' competition** – have previously (Porter 1985) been regarded as deciding the "BM organization in the industry" and thereby in our term the "BMES culture" – according to Porter the degree of rivalry between Businesses BM's.

However, as can be seen previous cluster and industry terminologies were very much defined as related to **the business** and **a single business.** However, our proposed framework "goes a step deeper than the business level". We argue that a business always has more than one business model (Lindgren, Horn Rasmussen 2013). Besides, the BMES terminology is related to the BM and the manifold of BM's that a business really have and potentially can create. Our different case studies indicates rather strong that a business is seldom represented with the whole business in just one BMES – all their BM's in one BMES – but with "parts of the business" – one or more BM's – in one BMES and other BM's in different BMESs.

5.3 The Black Box II and an Eco-System Approach

How do we get closer to a more methodological operational approach where theory can be absorbed into the analysis, explanation and understanding of BMI of today? Many researchers have studied the implicit or explicit assumptions around business models (Magretta 2002, Afuah 2003, Morris, Schindehutte & Allen 2005, Osterwalder, Pigneur & Tucci 2005, Chesbrough 2007, Lindgren, Taran & Boer 2010, Zott, Amit & Massa 2011, Markides 2013, Teece 2010). However, there is still not any acknowledge classification of BM. How is the situation with the idea of the links between BM, BMI and Eco Systems?

What do leading academics tell us about eco-systems and its link to business models and business model innovation? We will proceed with some examples.

The 2013 article "Business Model Innovation: What can the Ambidexterity Literature Teach Us?" (Markides 2013) don't even mention the term ecosystem and consequently the object for BMI is taken for given. Contrary to e.g. Markides, Zott and Amit (Zott, Amit 2013) have a focus on the idea of ecosystems. They argue: "The ecosystem concept could be viewed as closely related to the notion of the business model because it recognizes the need to go beyond a focal firm's boundaries and adopt a more systemic perspective that emphasizes interdependencies and complementarities between a firm and third parties in order to properly understand how value is created. Yet, in contrast to a business model, an ecosystem is not anchored on a focal firm; different firms can share the same ecosystem, yet have very different business models". On the one side they create a focus and a link between BM and ecosystems. On the other hand – even they indicate that we are dealing with boundaries – they only put a focus on an inside-out perspective – From business level and out to an ecosystem. They still are in a position where they treat a business as a BM and not as a business with many and co-existing business models within a business. And this is a crucial position because it will affect the point of departure for dealing with BMI. It is underlined in their definition of a business model: "We define a company's business model as a system of interconnected and interdependent activities that determines the way the company "does business" with its customers, partners and vendors. In other words, a business model is a bundle of specific activities—an activity system—conducted to satisfy the perceived needs of the market, along with the specification of which parties (a company or its partners) conduct which activities, and how these activities are linked to each other" (Amit, Zott 2012, page 42). Exactly the missing down-oriented dis-aggregation reflects how and where our framework differs.

Indirectly we find support for the need to also work with dis-aggregation (Shuen, Feiler & Teece 2014, Teece 2014).:

Only business processes and business models that yield value-enhancing differentiation constitute genuine dynamic capabilities. Such processes are usually quite unique and firm specific and may be thought of as "signature processes" or "signature business models." These arise from the firm's organizational heritage and so are difficult for competitors to imitate . . . . Strong ordinary capabilities are built on best practices; dynamic capabilities are built on signature practices and employ differentiated business models. Signature practices arise from a company's heritage and business models, including its prior management actions and context-specific learning (Shuen, Feiler & Teece 2014, page 7).

In the quote there is an explicit statement in order to work differentiated with the idea of business models. However, it is not clear whether the authors – like us – operates with the assumption that a business always have multiple business models? When they link to the idea of ecosystems we indirectly get indications for a confirming answer:

"They must generate and implement organizational and managerial innovations, both internally and within their ecosystems, to capture opportunities, overcome challenges, mitigate risks and achieve and sustain competitiveness". (Shuen, Feiler & Teece 2014, page 11).

The confirmation is rather indirectly and may be because of their explicit focus on the idea of capabilities and having another research goal than our very specific research goal?

However, in a recent litterature Teece (Teece 2015) may be claimed to have a more firm interpretation of the idea of an ecosystem and its relation to a business. Here we have a clear business level perspective (within the Teece universe he uses the notion of a firm level perspective.

"While the business enterprise plays a large role in determining the rate, direction, and nature of the commercially relevant technological change, the firm's ecosystem, including supporting institutions and legal structures, remains of great importance too, but is omitted in much theorizing about enterprise performance." (Teece 2015, page 681).

Teece is talkning about a firm's ecosystem, which clearly indicates an absent of understanding of e.g. the existence of different ecosystems related to a single business. A core in our framework and consequently a theoretial hard core in the Lakatos sense is the assumption of the potential for a business to have relations to different ecosystems. Teece illustrate his theoretical understanding of an ecosystem in a model termed: The Innovation Ecosystem. We interpret as a clear co-evolutionary model known from e.g. Norgaard (Norgaard 1994). We are talking about a "Spaghetti-model" where "The Innovating Enterprise" is placed in the middle and the surrounding environment consists of 8 virables. All the variable are connected with each other and all the variables are connceted with "The Innovation Enterprise". A change in one variable may or may not influence the other variable and "The Innovationg Enterprise". The variable of Teece are:

1. Supplieres and complementors
2. Regulatory and standards bodies
3. Financial Institutions
4. Human Capital
5. Rival firms
6. Government and Judiciary
7. Customer markets
8. Research Educational Institutions

While Teece clearly have a firm level focus – and what we pronounce a top-down analytical point of departure – his believe in the idea of eco-system and its importance is rather high even the idea has been scarcely used:

"Economic historians have always given considerable weight to the role of institutions and government in economic growth at the national level but very few studies connect the performance of particular firms to key elements in the ecosystem. However, vignettes and anecdotes abound. In the US civilian aircraft industry, for example, foreign technology and government procurement were vital inputs to domestic innovation. Boeing and others in the United States accessed developments in jet engine technology that had occurred in the United Kingdom and Germany in the creation of their own aircraft .... Boeing leveraged its subsequent success with the KC-130 jet tanker built for the Air Force into a civilian version—the Boeing 707— and captured a lead in global market share that lasted until the emergence and growth of Airbus. The nascent semiconductor industry also benefited from the willingness of the US military to buy advanced products at premium prices...........

Another prominent example of the ecosystem impacting innovation is the Internet. The basic technology and structure of the Internet has its origins in university research applied in the late 1960s by Bolt, Beranek, and Newman, a contractor to the US Department of Defense, to build a network connecting researchers with government contracts to government-sponsored computers in order to maximize resource utilization. ARPANET gradually extended its reach around the world and was merged in 1983 with similar networks to form the Internet" (Teece 2015, pages 686–687).

If we go back to the root of the idea of ecosystems in popular and practice oriented management theory, it was launched by James F. Moore in a McKinsey Award-winning article in 1993 presented in Harvard Business Review (Moore 1993). His point of departure was: "I suggest that a company be viewed not as a member of a single industry but as part of a *business ecosystem* that crosses a variety of industries. In a business ecosystem, companies co-evolve capabilities around a new innovation: they work cooperatively and competitively to support new products, satisfy customer needs, and eventually incorporate the next round of innovations (p. 76)." Moore continued to evolve on the idea and qualified it (Moore 1996, Moore 1998, Moore 2006). A main point in the works of Moore is his focus on business inter-organizational relevance or with his words: ".... These extended systems of mutually supportive organizations" (Moore 1998, page 168). Having an innovation perspective Moore points at the need to move focus from the classical and traditional M-form organization to a rise of an E-form organization. It is a question of – in our terms – "Where to Look". He puts it this way:

"The problem with this sort of organization is that through its focus on core operations, it creates in managers a corresponding blindness to developments that happen outside of one's core. That is, managers find it difficult to attend to the so-called "white space" between existing markets and operations. Yet in a global economy with ample free capital, management talent, and technological inventiveness, much of the opportunity facing businesses originates in the white space" (p. 174).

And he elaborates it further:

"The new corporation must be centrally engaged in market and industry creation, whether to extend or to replace its existing enterprises. Market and industry creation – the establishment of new business ecosystems – is giving rise to new forms of corporate leadership and structure. Form, after all, follows function. The multidivisional form is giving way to the ecosystemic form. E-form organizations focus on markets and potential markets. The E-form organization differs from its M-form competitors in two major ways:

First, for each business ecosystem in which the corporation has an interest, the E-form organization is geared to address the total range of ecosystem leadership issues—and not just those of its operating businesses that serve the ecosystem. The E-form organization self-consciously leads a community of allies. Second, to the extent that an E-form enterprise has interests in multiple ecosystems, it can coordinate its cross-ecosystem activities and participate in ecosystems with a diversity of developmental challenges." (p. 174–175).

Like Zott and Amit, Moore operates primarily at a business level and with an inside-out perspective.

In 2006 Moore as a member of the American Antitrust Institute roundtable on Complexity, Networks, and the Modernization of Antitrust contributed with the article "Business ecosystems and the view from the firm" in Antitrust Bulletin (Moore 2006). A main point within our context is his argumentation around how the existing pratical, theoretical and political missing focus on the existence of ecosystems leads to legislation that is far behind the need of reality. *"For more than sixty years, markets and hierarhcies have dominated our thinking about economic organization . . . . . . Markets, hierarchies, and ecosystems are the three pillars of modern business thinking and should provide the foundation for competition policy, regulation, and antitrust actions"* (p. 31). One of the consequences of the missing involvement of the ecosystems notion is that existing legislation may damage instead of create the framework conditions for business innovation: *"Given this framing of the situation, the remedies can include rigid, imposed independence at particular interfaces within an ecosystem and a resulting breakdown in co-evolutionary exchanges necessary for innovation. The unhappy results are the imposition of profound social costs attendant to sloved innovation. Unfortunately, these costs are hidden because they result from a future denied, rather than from a present destroyed"* (p. 48).

Part of "The Moore-Universe" can be expressed with reference to DeLong (DeLong 2000), who defined business ecology as "a more productive set of processes for developing and commercializing new technologies" that is characterized by the "rapid prototyping, short product-development cycles, early test marketing, options-based compensation, venture funding, early corporate independence".

5.4 The Black Box II and a Business Model Eco-System (BMES) Approach

Even the theoretical approach of Moore operates at a business level it fits well with our proposals. Especially because our idea of operating with the Cube at an eco-system level fits well into the framework elaborated by Moore.

By definition and with reference to the theoretical "Moore-Universe" we propose analogically a BMES as: *A "community of living BM's" where different businesses offer their "AS IS BM" and develop their "TO BE BM" in conjunction with the BMES environment."* In this context and in our approach BM's that are under construction is also "living" BM's in the BMES as these use resources of the BMES on innovating these. The consequence of our offering is two-fold.

First, we distinguish to other frameworks (Porter e.g.) by focusing on the BM's and not the Business as forming the BMES. We argue that Business offers their BM's to the BMES – but very seldom their total amount of BM's and thereby their total business to a BMES. In our research (Windmill BMES, Valvet BMES, Fair BMES, Building BMES, Furniture BMES, Food BMES and FOOD TECH BMES, Energy BMES) we found that Business seldom offered all their BM's in just one BMES. Business is most often spreading their BM's to more BMES – to gain more business, spread risk strategically or because of other reasons. Our research show that Business who offer all or nearly all their BM's to one BMES often face large strategy risk, are easier to set under value and cost pressure by customers, suppliers and competitors. The strategic best practice sentence" – "Stick to Your core business" (Abell 1980) is therefore maybe not fully true in all business contexts because the business can be strategically trapped in one BMES by doing so. The strategic best practice sentence "focus on Your core competence" (Prahalad, Hamel 1990) can be true, when a business offers the same value proposition to more BMES – but can be strategically risky if the BMES context based changes.

Second, we distinguish to most industry, sector and cluster research, as they do not consider and included the "TO BE" BM as part of the BMES – or what they call a market (Kotler, Armstrong 2010, Kotler 1983) or Industry (Porter 1985). We argue that "TO BE" BM's are equal important part and valuable to any BMES or to many BMES as there is e.g. customers, suppliers and value proposition that are "flowing" into and out from the BMES and hereby influence highly the BMES although these BM's are not fully developed. As an example we found that "TO BE" APPS development and new gaming software development in Silicon Valley incubation environment are influencing the "AS IS" BM's in the APPS – and software BMES – and some of these "TO BE" BM'S are even "traded" before final launch – at concept phase and even at the initial idea phase.

We acknowledge that many business – and also societies – put their primary focus on the BMES's "AS IS" BM's – but we point to that this is not giving the full picture and understanding of all dimensions and characteristics of a BMES if the "TO BE" BM's is not included in the BMES. The "TO BE" BM's and the proposed "TO BE BM's" indeed influences and "value" the rest of the BMES BM's. Businesses use tremendous resources from the BMES and other BMES to carry out their BMI or to protect their "AS IS" BM's from "TO BE" BM's. "TO BE" BM's can be serious and important drivers to change of "AS IS" BM's in the BMES and can simply be the source to changing a BMES – and its vertically (implementing BMI across different eco-systems) and horizontal (implementing BMI within a specific eco-system) related BMES. Amazone, Itunes and Netflix are just some examples of business that have influenced highly classic and previously conservative BMES in retail, music and film. "TO BE" BM's can even disrupt a BMES and sometimes be the drivers to destruct BMES or related BMES. "TO BE" BM's can even be the driver to the establishment of new BMES (e.g. Second Life, World of Warcraft, The Tinder Box Festival in Denmark (Tinderbox.dk)).

Physical boarders like land, countries and continents have for many years been regarded as boarders to markets, industries, sectors, clusters and even businesses. Digital and virtual boarders in cyperspace as Google Search, Apple Itunes, Blizzard – World of Warcraft, Zynga – Farmvillage, Viasat TV platform,TDC mobile network are just some examples of BMES, which follows different boarders – digital and virtual boarders. Some digital and virtual BMES are free to access Google Search, Wikipedia – others are not Disney World Paris, Legoland Billund but digital and virtual BMES do often not stick to the physical boarders of yesterday and push us to change over previous understanding of markets, industry, sectors and clusters.

Kotler (Kotler, Armstrong 2010) (Kotler 1983) described a market as consisting of values offered to customers to fulfill their wants, needs and demands. Markets consisting of customers and suppliers, who exchange values (products and service) for money. Markets with market leaders and markets followers competing and preventing new entrants to enter the market. Kotler also described markets as those with special demands for value "niche markets" and those with indifferent demands "mass markets". All as small BMES – ecosystem or communities with special or indifferent value demands. The customers value demand and the supplier's value offers as boarders for "the ecosystem" and the money as the final determinant of whether a market exists or not.

Porter (Porter 1985) described it somehow differently. He defined any industry related to entry and exit barriers – "Borders" – to their industry. "Exit barriers" – preventing business to slip out of the industry and "entry barriers" preventing substitutes and new entrants to slip into the industry. Obstacles that make it both difficult to exit and enter a given industry. Hindrances that a business faces in trying to exit and enter an industry with its BM's— such as capital investment, government regulations, taxes and patents, or a large, established Business taking advantage of economies of scale— or those lack of competences a Business faces in trying to gain entrance to a profession—such as technology requirements, education or licensing requirements, organizational requirements or cultural practice. Because entry barriers protect incumbent businesses and restrict competition in an industry, they can contribute to distortionary value formulas. The existence of monopolies or industry power is often aided to barriers to entry – and thereby "the boarders" to an industry.

Following both Kotler and Porter and translate it to a description of "Ecosystems" we will have keywords as special habits, rules, practice – "culture" (Kotler 1983) – B2C markets, B2B markets, (Porter 1985) – rivalry, cost leaders, niche and focus strategist. However, the business environment seems in many cases only to be true if these boarders really exists and we claim that they might not be existing any more. It seems that they have changed or even vanished since the early 1980es especially with the internet pushing and disrupting boarders of markets, industries, sectors and clusters. The internet also providing the opportunity to act in physical, digital and virtual BMES simultaneously or integrated.

So to answer the question – what are the boarders to a BMES it might be valuable to rethink the term barriers and borders – and instead think as context based. Consequently, we indicate that the boarders of ecosystems depend on the context and the viewpoint. Successful BMES in the future may have to be established and look different from those we know of the past. The approach to the term BMES and our viewpoint to BMES may have to be seen differently than as previous terms like industry, sector and cluster surrounded and related to physical and geographical boarders. Context boarders and approaches might be giving us different and even better strategic advantage to previous terms. A deeper and new understanding of BMES could give some different and new answers to why some BMES are successful and others not – and why a BMES terminology that is more context based defined could be valuable to future BMI.

5.5 Eco-System Construction

As the above argumentation strongly indicates, it is our interpretation that the ecosystem perspective contributes to the discussion about global business innovation and makes it more operational from a practical perspective. Heikkilä and Kuivaniemi (Heikkilä, Kuivaniemi 2012) illustrates in their article "Ecosystem under construction: An action Research study on entrepreneurship in a business ecosystem" how the two black boxes can be folded out and how such picture can assist in practice in business model innovation process. The model is inspired by Moore (Moore 1993, Moore 1996) and indicates their understanding of a business ecosystem.

They operate at three levels of abstraction or "different layers", where their point are that the longer distance we are from the core business level the less commitment we have to business. The three levels are:

- System level.
- Extended business level.
- Core business level.

Related to Lundvall we see that the idea of a core level is important. However, here the wider settings – if we again should compare with Lundvall – are defined by two different levels – extended business level and system level. The three levels consist on different contents which they illustrate in the following model.

5.5.1 The Finnish business ecosystem model

The researchers argue: "The core business layer consists of the parties forming the heart of the business. In traditional business, this layer would be run

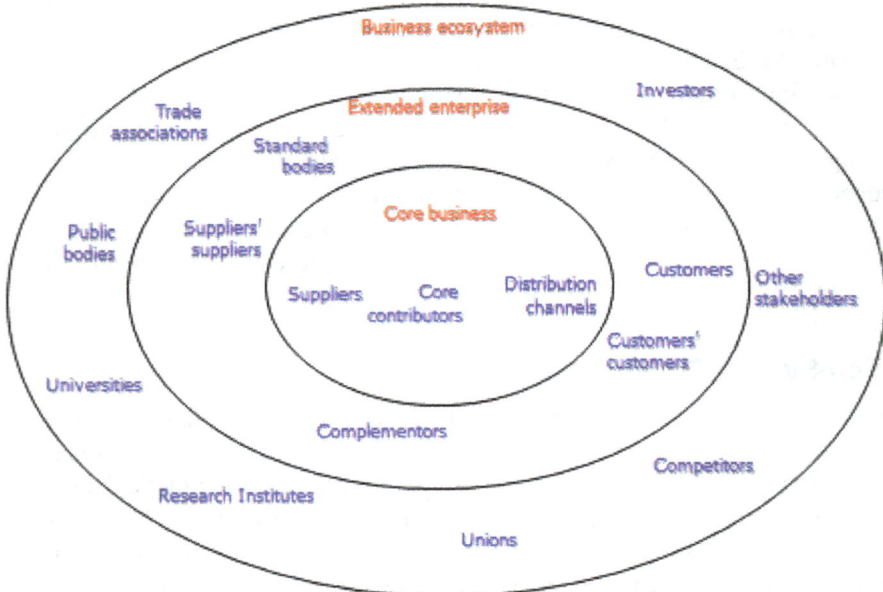

Figure 5   The Finish Eco-System Model I.

Source: (Heikkilä, Kuivaniemi 2012).

by a single company[9] or the supply chain would be coordinated by the focal company. Alternatively, it can also be formed by a network of several companies each taking care of part of the core business. The next layer, the extended enterprise, widens the view of the business supply chain to widens the view of the business supply chain to include customers, complementors and second-layer suppliers, as well as standard-setting bodies in particular field of business. The outermost layers add trade associations, unions, universities and stakeholders to the business eco-system" (Heikkilä, Kuivaniemi 2012, page 19). Such are their definitions of the landscape from which an innovation occurs and becomes an integrated part of the core business. And precisely their description of the landscape forms an active role in the process of construction of an eco-system for innovations.

Their point of departure is similar with our purpose, because they also have observed how practitioners point out that "it is rather easy to come up with new ideas, but the real challenge is to put them into practice" (Heikkilä, Kuivaniemi 2012, page 18). A major reason for this has a reference to the complexity of the surroundings. In their perspective the task is to concentrate the efforts around the innovation. "Instead, an ecosystem consisting of multiple expertises, capabilities and resources should be created around the innovation"—where "The aim is to recognize the different domains of players that are or should be involved in the ecosystem under construction" (do).

The Finnish Business Ecosystem Model – From Phase 0 to Phase 2

Based upon a concrete case – Physical Activity Prescription, a service innova-tion in preventive healthcare – they demonstrates why earlier efforts with the concrete case failed and how another perspective take over the business model innovation process. This is illustrated in the next model. Phase 0 is the earlier efforts which had focus around the public sector and research institutions. Institutions placed in the outer layer compared with the core of the innovation. Phase 0 was public financed and the efforts to innovate stopped after funding stopped. Phase 1 is the situation when an entrepreneur took over. Point of departure was identification of actors who had a commercial interest in the new innovation. The key players identified by the entrepreneur were private

---

[9]Remark that we consequently use the term business instead of company. One of the reasons are that any business consist of more than one business model. We want to create a focus on the black box one as a box with more than one business model. This has fundamental consequences when a business address attention toward BMI-processes.

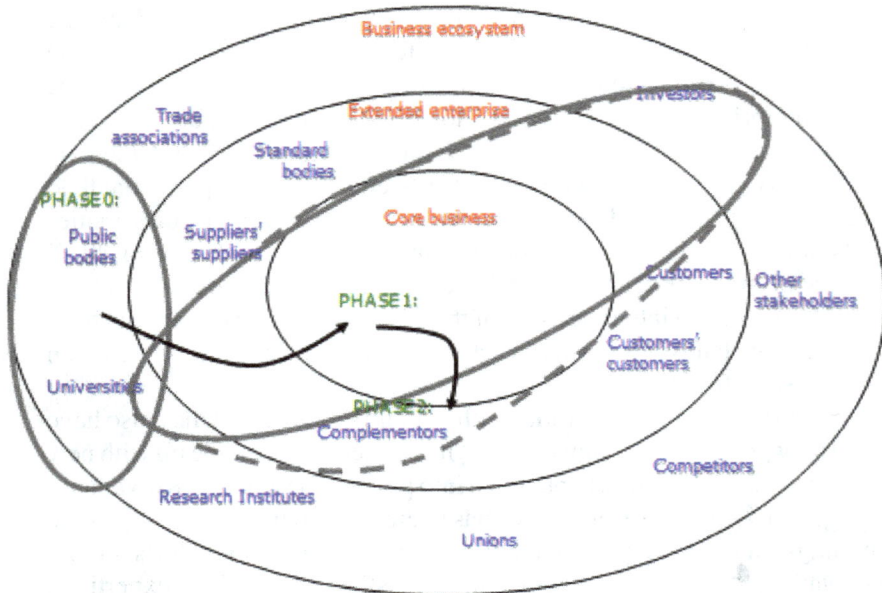

Figure 6   The Finish Eco-System Model II.

Source: (Heikkilä, Kuivaniemi 2012).

medical clinics, pharmacies and the entrepreneurs own company. The value add in the new model comes from "an entirely new process consisting of tasks carried out in multiple organizations" (Heikkilä, Kuivaniemi 2012, page 22). However, phase 2 is where the project was in June 2012, because the question of the implementation of the innovation rest upon how to use new information technology and there is a need to build a prototype – proof of concept. This involves different business negotiation with information systems providers and health monitoring equipment suppliers.

As indicated much efforts and the starting point in the innovation strategy was concentrated far from the core of the core business. Based upon their research, literature and different workshops the researchers identified actual names on the potential players related to the innovation. Then they rearranged their former models and organized it with respect to sub-ecosystems. Their claim is that this model has a generic character (Horn Rasmussen 2013). We shortly present and comment on this model, which presents a new kind of seeing the landscape for innovation activities.

The Finnish Generic Sub-Ecosystems within the Business Ecosystem

Their model calls for two main points. First we have 6 different areas where the innovation activity must put attention. However, they don't comment whether we have potential actors at all the three levels in the different sub-systems. However and second, a main argument and point in their model is that they incorporate the notion of time – or as they pronounce it: clock-speed – in their model. They have arranged the sub-ecosystems with those systems with the highest velocity to the right – technological change – and the slowest to the left – policies and legal environment. According to their recommendations any innovation activity must pay attention to any of the sub-systems in its planning. While most of the sub-systems doesn't need further introduction we need explicit attention on their idea about co-opetition. This notion covers the situation where competitors become a collaborator. The reasons can be many.

The models do in many ways enrich the idea of a national innovation system, because we find it goes a bit deeper into the concrete context from a

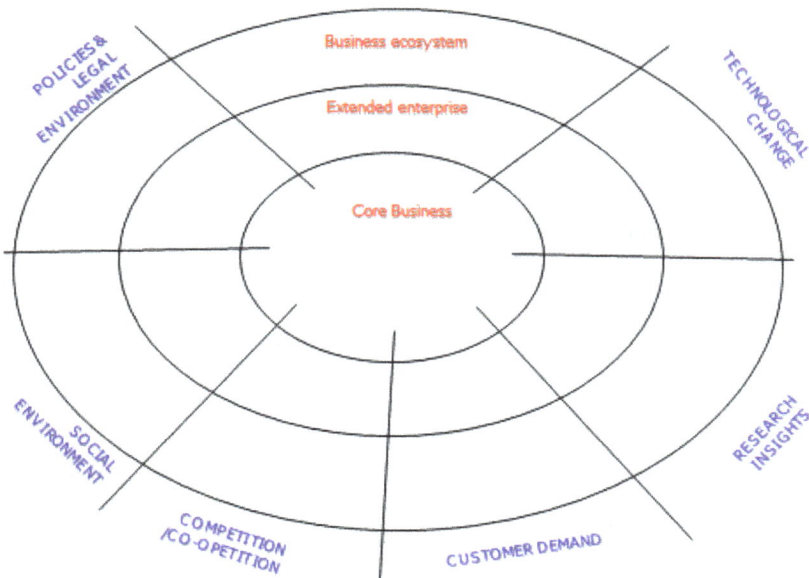

Figure 7   The Finish Eco-System Model III.

Source: Heikkilä & Kuivaniemi (2012).

microeconomic point of view. However, and we will argue for it, the models are still mostly inspired of the top-down or macroeconomic perspective. Even focus is the entrepreneur. This means that the models most of all call attention on what we initially named "The Black Box II" or the surroundings of the business. We are going to go more deeply and the task has reference to "The Black Box I". The work of Heikkilä and Kuivaniemi contributes to a broader understanding of the innovations landscape, on the importance of different sub-areas, the idea of co-option and maybe most important the need to incorporate the idea of time and the different velocity or clock-speed that the different sub-systems represents, because all this influences if or if not the innovation becomes a reality and a successful or an un-successful innovation.

6 Synthesis – The Importance of Different Levels of Abstraction – The Vertical Butterfly as a Hard Core in the theoretical Framework of Business Models, Business Model Innovation and Business Model Eco-Systems

6.1 The Three BM Archetypes, the CUBE and Eco-Systems

Any attempt to qualify the discussion of the idea of business model may as a point of departure take into account the idea of using the term "business model" at different levels of abstraction. So far we have identified at least 3 BM archetypes – two microeconomic and one macroeconomic archetype:

1. **A macroeconomic archetype:** Business model as a long term reflection about how the economy is organized at a macro-level, among nations and among groups of nations.

Lazonick (Lazonick 2010, page 677) points it out this way:

"As Alfred Chandler documented in The Visible Hand (1977), by the 1920s the managerial revolution in American capitalism had transformed the organization of the economy. Over the next half-century, the "Chandlerian" corporation put in place what I have called the "old-economy business model," characterized by oligopolistic competition, career employment with one company, and regulated financial markets. From the 1980s, however, this model began to break down, in part because of its own "financial-ization," which began with the conglomerate movement of the 1960s, and in part because of the rise of Japanese competition, starting in the 1970s.

The Japanese competed successfully against the Americans in automobiles, consumer electronics, microelectronics, machine tools, and steel, industries in which the U.S. companies had been the world's leading mass producers. In effect, as I will argue in this essay, Japan outperformed the United States by perfecting the old-economy model". .... *Led by Intel and its microprocessor for the IBM personal computer (PC) and its clones, U.S. companies became world leaders in chip design. Indeed, the IBM PC and its "Wintel" architecture laid the basis for the rise of what I have called the "new-economy business model," which by the year 2000 had relegated the old-economy model to history* .... *A particular business model is defined by its strategy, organization, and finance. The contrasting strategic, organizational, and financial characteristics of the new- and old-economy models developed initially in the information and communication technology industries, as laid out in Table 1. Of particular importance to the rise of the new-economy model was the change in employment relations within high-tech sectors* ...... *the rise of the new-economy business model elevated the stock market to a position of far greater influence over the allocation of resources to innovative enterprise than it had occupied before* .... *The separation of ownership from control occurs to some extent under the new-economy business model when companies list on the stock market. Under this more recent paradigm, however, the stock market also performs compensation and combination functions. Through the offer of what came to be known as "broad-based" stock-option plans, the rise of the new-economy model relied for its success on prospective stockmarket gains to induce professional, technical, and administrative labor to leave secure employment at established companies for insecure employment at startups."*

Our point bringing such a long presentation by Lazonick is that it documents the relevance operating with the idea of business model at a macroeconomic level of abstraction. However, the use of model made by Lazonick underlines his long term time perspective. As documented in Horn Rasmussen (Horn Rasmussen 2008) separation of ownership and control is far from a new event and far from a new paradigm. Horn Rasmussen describes how the American economist Thorstein Veblen 100 years ago introduced the change in how the organization of the economic operates – and in this context we may refer to this as a fundamental change in the business model – both with reference to the single business and the economy as a whole. However, we find that the analysis of Lazonick is a well capable description of how to operate with the idea of business model at a macroeconomic level.

2. **Microeconomic archetype I:** Business model as a term which is most
   adequate and analogue to a business.
3. **Microeconomic archetype II:** Business model as a part of a business,
   which per definition contains of more than one Business Model.

Archetype 2 and 3 can be presented within the framework of The Business
Model Cube (Lindgren, Horn Rasmussen 2013). However, the definition of
the Cube can also work at higher level of abstraction – a national level, an eco-
system level and within the highest level of abstraction – a global economic
level. Consequently, we argue that "The Cube" in theory and practice represent
a methodology which can be used at many levels of abstraction – From
what we could term "Micro-Micro-Micro" (BM-level) to "Meta-Level" (The
Global Economy Level). In the following we will outline the content in the
way of thinking and the way of understanding.

The Cube is characterized by its 7 dimension – where the relations so to
speak – kits the other six dimensions. By this procedure we get our CUBE.

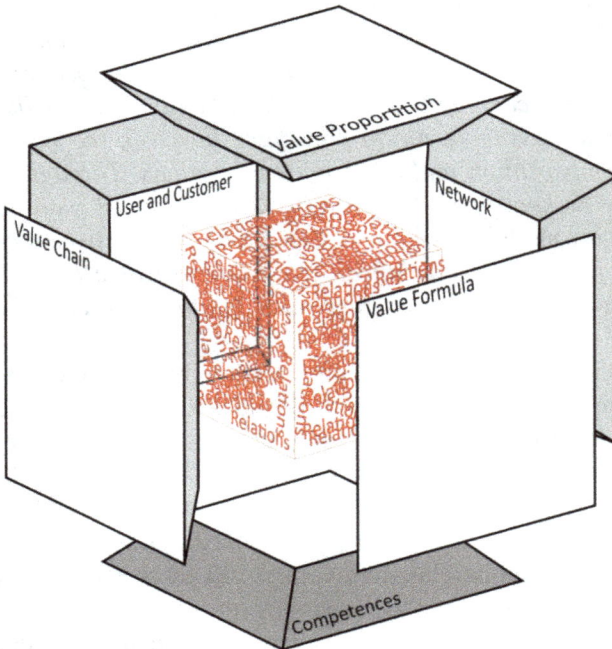

Figure 8   The Cube.

Source: (Lindgren, Horn Rasmussen 2013).

The Cube is a definition. How does the CUBE operate with reference to Black Box I? Most simple it is a definition of a business. However – as pointed out above, the Cube as definition can operate at different levels of abstraction – from a business model level, to a portfolio level of business models and to a business level. The CUBE's can be dis-aggregated into 6 specific dimensions and the seventh dimension, the relations, which kit the blocks together. The dimensions can be further divided into different components and in some of the dimensions also sub-components. Black Box I can be illustrated in this simple way where Black Box II – The Surroundings of the Business now is replaced by the term Eco-System Level.

When we use the CUBE with reference to Black Box II we are going to argue and elaborate Black Box II step by step.

In our terminology we first concentrate on type 3. Type 2 is hardly a new issue and we use type 2 in order to define type 3. However, and this is important, the inclusion of type 1 is necessary, because this is here we get a reference to the idea of an eco-system which is a concept we from a macroeconomic perspective know from ecological economics and e.g. launched by Costanza et.al. (Costanza et al. 1997). From a business perspective we find the idea of an ecosystem e.g. within marketing theory. The relevance of the concept

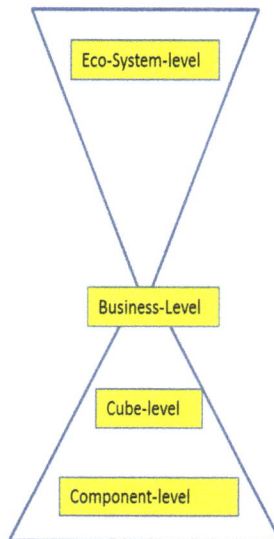

Figure 9 First Edition of the Vertical Butterfly – Black Box 2 Defined as the Eco-System Level and Black Box 1 Defined Using the Cube Methodology.

Source: (Horn Rasmussen 2013 (January)).

is e.g. expressed by John G. Singer, founder and principal of Blue Spoon Consulting Group, LLC, Minneapolis, USA. Singer (2006: 50) states:

"Advantage goes to those marketers who do the better job of designing ecosystems with mutually-reinforcing effects from internal and external assets, and managing the ecosystems for growth, innovation, and continual improvement".

With other words: The idea of ecosystems is rather crucial for any business and we are going to contribute on how a business can exploit the concrete ecosystems within the process of Business Model Innovation. However, dealing with ecosystems and the theory behind it, we are moving into a really cross disciplinary arena where e.g. theory of biological systems, theory of ecology, evolutionary and co-evolutionary theory, network theory and marketing theory creates its own not well defined framework for a complex, ever changing system which are irreversible. As it turns out the demands to management and leadership in any business becomes both complex and challenging.

Our mission is in many ways similar to the Finnish researchers. Theoretically we also work with the combination of an inductive and deductive methodology.

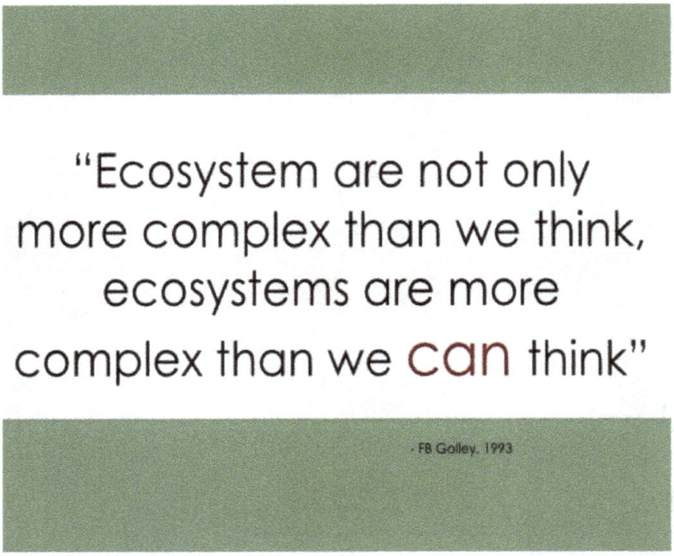

"Ecosystem are not only more complex than we think, ecosystems are more complex than we **can** think"

- FB Golley. 1993

Figure 10   An Interesting Hypothesis from the Ecologist and Philosopher FB Golley.

6.2 Theoretical Point of Departure in Schumpeter: Contributions to the Theoretical Hard Core and Its Practical Approach for Business Model Innovation

Our point of departure is the ideas about definitions formulated by Schumpeter. First of all we will abstract from the fact that Schumpeter only pronounce the idea of products, while his followers also speak about the idea of service and processes of products and services as value propositions from a BM. However within Schumpeters theoretical world service can also be argued to be a product. However and this is important we have to see at a central distinction in his framework.

"To produce means to combine materials and forces within our reach. To produce other things, or the same things by a different method, means to combine these materials and forces differently. In so far as the "new combination" may in time grow out of the old by continuous adjustment in small steps, there is certainly change, possibly growth, but neither a new phenomenon nor development in our sense. In so far as this is not the case, and the new combinations appear discontinuously, then the phenomenon characterizing development emerges. For reasons of expository convenience, henceforth, we shall only mean the latter case when we speak of new combinations of productive means. Development in our sense is then defined by the carrying out of new combinations" (Schumpeter 1983 (1934), pages 65–66).

This concept, Schumpeter argues, covers 5 cases. Casadesus-Manasell et al. (Casadesus-Masanell, Ricart 2010) – with explicit reference to Schumpeter – names these as five types of innovations:

1. new product,
2. new methods of production,
3. new sources of supply,
4. exploitation of new markets, and
5. new ways to organize business

Casadesus-Manasell argues that much of the literature so far has focused on the first two types of innovation. However, their study focuses on the last type of innovation, which they claim often is referred to as business model innovation. They state that Business model innovation has become increasingly important both in academic literature and in practice given the increasing number of opportunities for business model configurations enabled by technological progress, new customer preferences, and deregulation. They further argue that BMI, at root, refers to the search for new logics of the firm (remark they don't use the term: business), new ways to create and capture value for its stakeholders, and focuses primarily on finding new ways to generate revenues and define value propositions for customers, suppliers, and partners Further they state that business model innovation often affects the whole enterprise (remark they don't use the term: business).

Our interpretation of Schumpeter challenge Casadesus-Manasell. Based upon Schumpeter and our research we claim that:

1. A business contains at root two archetypes of BMs. AS-IS Business models and To-Be Business models. The AS-IS BM operates at the penetrated market (Kotler 1983), whereas the TO BE BM focus at both the penetrated market, served market, available market, qualified available and potential market (Kotler 1983).
2. Business model innovation has its reference to both kind of models mentioned in point one.
3. Business Model Innovation is about any kind of innovation within the seven dimensions of the CUBE.
4. Business model innovation – at root and in accordance to e.g. Casadesus-Masanell and Ricart – refers also to how to organize the different business models in a business or in a BMES.
5. Business model innovation – at root – refers to reorganization of the different business models in the business with reference to both a monetary and a non-monetary value formula in the business.
6. Business model innovation must have assistance from different tools in order to reach optimal results in the process.
7. Downloading – Seeing – and Sensing represent the main techniques in such process.
8. The Cube organizes the process and secure a certain order.
9. Different tools like the relation axiom organize the certain order into different perspectives.

6.3 The Frameworks Understanding of Black Box II – Part One

We now proceed with our presentation of our content of the Black Boxes – starting looking from a microeconomic and business point of view – *we go down – top* – In the efforts to define the content in the black boxes it is uncontroversial to argue that the idea of a relation between a business and an eco-system has different levels of abstraction.

1. Business Level has active Relations to the eco-system.
2. Business Level has Resting Relations to the eco-system[10].
3. Business Level has None Relations to the eco-system.

Now the notion relation has a similar function. The relation is the connection between a business and the eco-system. This can be illustrated as shown in Figure 11.

The first two levels of abstraction already is part of the business. However, the two levels are characterized by having two fundamental different positions – an active and an inactive position. The third position reflects elements, which is un-related to the business level. In order to bridge to the "normal" understanding of the interplay between a business and its

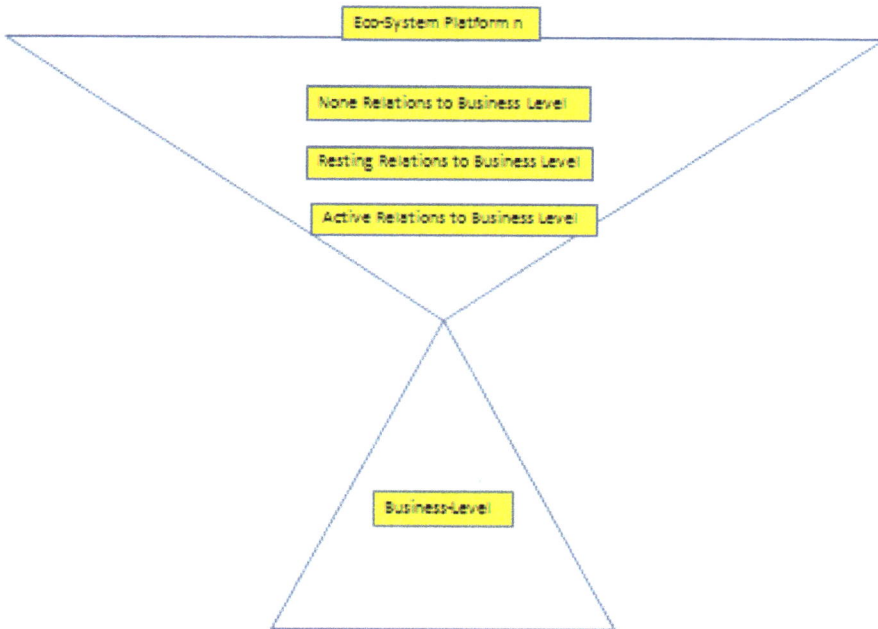

Figure 11 Black Box 2 as Eco-System Platform with or without Relations to Black Box 1 Defined as Business Level.

Source: (Horn Rasmussen, Lindgren & Saghaug 2014).

---

[10]Based upon our research we have found that it make sense – gives meaning – for a business to sub-divide this into resting relations to business level with a future potential and resting relation to business level which the business actively have chosen not to be potential for their BMI. The business knows the relation but has excluded the relation.

surroundings, we define the sum of all the three levels as the eco-system of the business. We could also name it as an eco-system platform.

If we connect the above model to the idea of Business Model Innovation, it is obviously that it becomes very important that the business is very aware of which level they are investigating and which level they so to speak build and model. Exactly the existence of the different levels is the first indicator for how wide a potential any business has with respect to its business model innovation activities. Besides, it is a clear indication that in order to exploit the potential there need to be implemented much mapping time and consequently much analytic time as well. The relation axiom is the first step toward the establishing of a connection between the BM and the BM-Eco-system. It is the relation-axiom, which creates the first kind of order and create a first foundation of description of the eco-system which it belongs to. The second indicator for the wide innovation potential in any business has reference to the fact, that any business may or may not interact with more than one eco-system. The photo in Figure 12 is from a workshop with 4 entrepreneurs in Skive, Denmark, October 2013 and illustrate the challenges for a business and its business models (Horn Rasmussen, Lindgren 2013).

As demonstrated we can talk about business models and business model innovation at different levels of abstraction. In order to be sure that we all are talking about the same, the model at the photo are outlined more "clean" beneath and may act as a guide. Originally we have got the inspiration from microeconomics and the discussion of the difference between transaction marketing and relationship marketing. Graphically it is illustrated with a butterfly and an inverse butterfly (Lindgreen et al. 2000). Inspired by the discussion, we name our model "The Vertical Butterfly". However, contrary to the distinction in the marketing concept between a butterfly and an inverse butterfly, our model doesn't have any distinctions and doesn't chose any concept. The model is just a description of how we see the potential object for a BMI process and how we want to organize ourselves before we start the business model innovation process. The model acts as a kind of theoretical memory card. In the practical work it is a matter of "driving in the right direction" within the different phases of the business model innovation process.

The general reflection and the rationale in the model tell that we can look upon a business from different perspectives of aggregation. In explanation of the model point of departure is the intersection point between the two triangles. We define the point as the level of a business. Going down from the point we disaggregate the business. When we go up into the eco-system

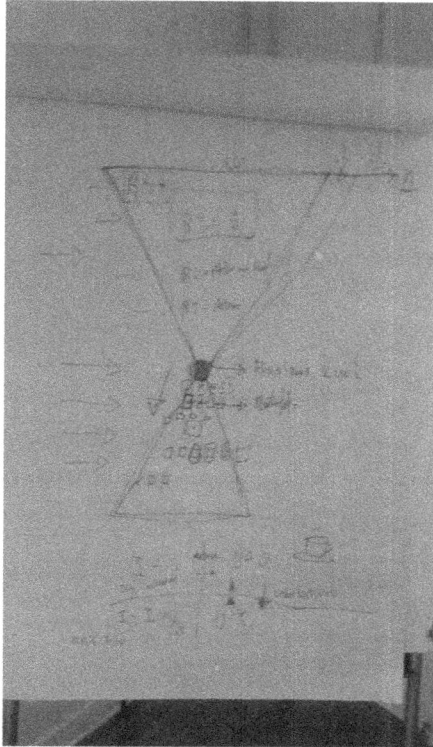

Figure 12 Workshop photo Vertical Butterfly, October 2013.

Source: (Horn Rasmussen, O. & Lindgren, P. 2013)

we aggregate[11]. As a matter of logic we are able to dis-aggregate and aggregate into different levels. In our context it make sense at least to disaggregate first into the portfolio of the business. Within our framework the portfolio is defined as the existing TO-BE and AS-IS Business Models grouped into categorizes. Some would argue that we are at the level of business. However, within our context it makes only sense to argue that our concept of AS-IS and TO-BE business models must be placed beyond the level of business, because this

---

[11] In this discussion we abstract from the theoretical discussion about the atomic fallacy even we find the arguments for the problematic issue of summing all the micro and claim we have macro for quite convincing. However, we find that in this context the discussion is non-relevant because of our heuristic, theoretical purpose of making an attempt to contribute to a theory of business models and business model innovation.

Eco-systems Platform 1

None Relations to Business Level

Resting Relations to Business Level

Active Relations to Business Level

Business Level

Business Model Portfolio Level

Business Model Level

Cube Dimension Level

Dimension Component Level

Dimension Sub-Component Level

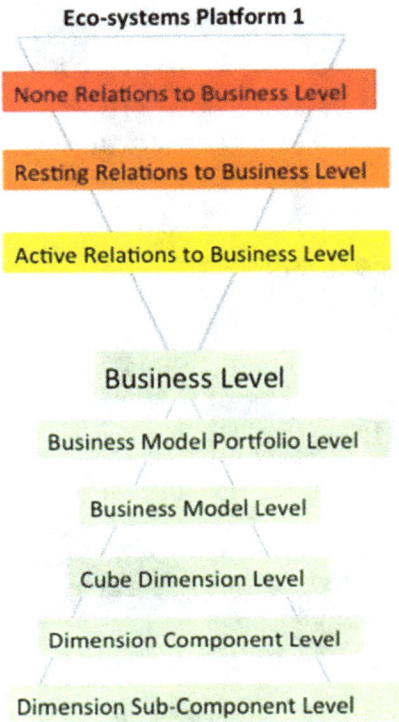

Figure 13 The Vertical Butterfly: Black Box 2 as Eco-System Platform 1 with or without Relations to Black Box 1 Defined at Six Levels of Abstraction.

level simply is characterized by different business models which put together are an expression of the business.

Expanding the model, we must imagine that we have different "Standing Butterflies" side by side. The point is that management who has such overview gets a lot richer, however also a more complex, picture of the business and consequently the business has a lot richer potential position for the business model innovation process. We claim that the potential for the business model innovation process strongly increases. Potentially, we in practice can operate at different levels of the vertical level of dis-aggregation but now also from a horizontal perspective – We so to speak will argue that a further horizontal dis-aggregation will open op for an inherent potential of business innovation. While the dis-aggregation from a business level to the level of business models and further down to components is characterized as a vertical dis-aggregation this dis-aggregation is characterized as a horizontal dis-aggregation. The model beneath illustrate the new situation.

The model illustrates, that the business – at a business level – may or may not be bound together with different eco-system platforms. We will argue that such perspective opens for new potentials for innovation for any current business and its business models. This includes all the TO-BE BM and their potential on its way into a market.

The "BMI Where to Look Model I" points out the importance to be aware about the following issue – which is evil relevant for any AS-IS BM and TO-BE BM:

There exist many levels of abstraction.

The important issue is: Which of the different levels of abstraction are in focus in the different phases of the downloading and seeing BMI process.

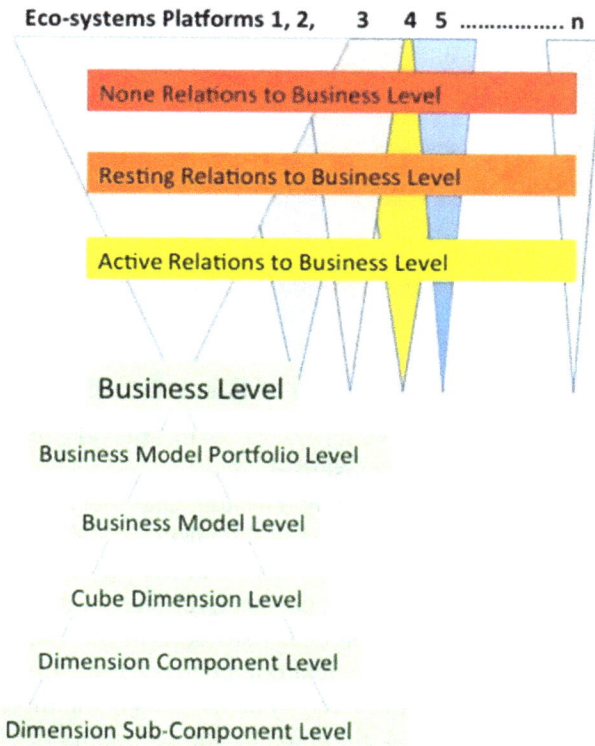

Figure 14 The Vertical Butterflies: Black Box 2 as Eco-System Platforms 1, 2, 3, 4, 5.......n with or without Relations to Black Box 1 Defined at Six Levels of Abstraction.

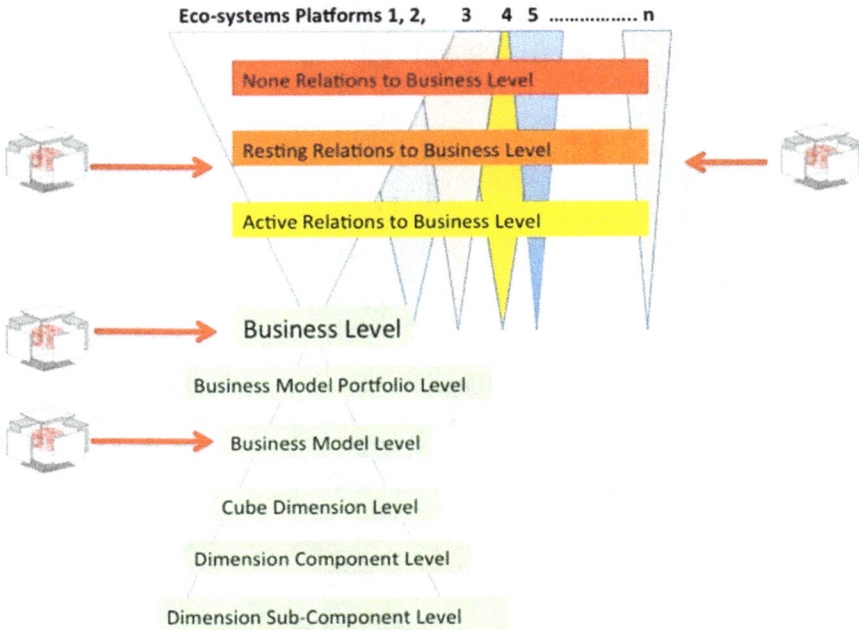

Figure 15   The Business Model Innovation "Where to Look Model I".

When it comes to the strategic scenario BMI process these considerations have equal importance.

6.4 The Frameworks Understanding of Black Box II – Part Two

What happens if we – instead of having focus at business level – remove focus to BM level? The idea is that there exist many eco-systems and the relevance from the business may alter as times go by. This indicates that an eco-system - when point of departure is a concrete BM in the business – always is unique and always is context dependent. Remark here that the position here is seen from the BM perspective – an inside out perspective. The point about context dependence may be part of the theoretical hard core in the Lakatos sense. The potential for any BM is from a logical point of view the global economy and consequently the total amount of eco-systems. This is the model around which everything revolves around. Summed up the second model which we use in practice and the model which present the second idea of "Where to Look?" is:

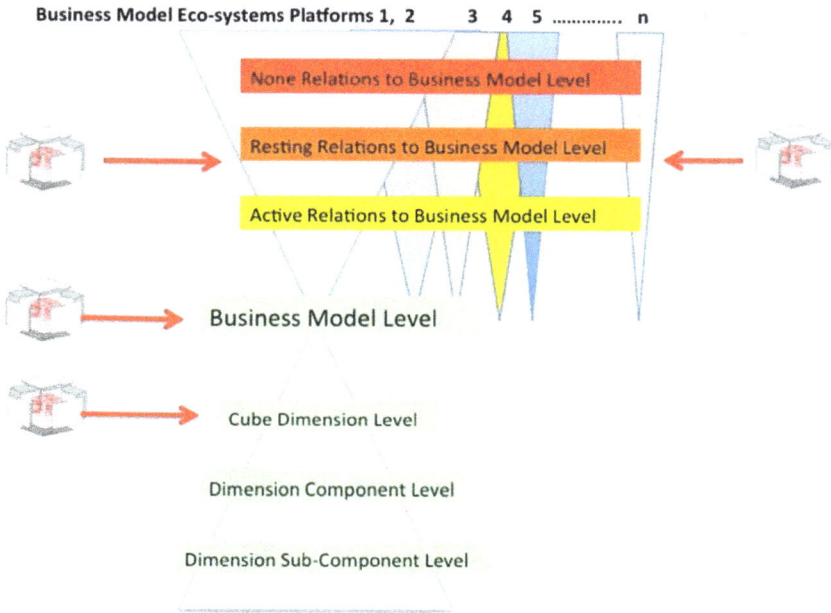

Figure 16 Where to Look Model II – The Real BM Business Model Innovation Context.

From the model we can see that business level has been deleted. Now the BM is placed in the vertical butterfly at the place where the business was placed. Consequently, in the model the business level now becomes part of the eco-systems. And instead of talking about eco-systems we now talks about Business Model Eco-Systems (BMES). This means that we have two models which any business should be aware of in their BMI processes. The one where focus is business level and the second where focus is BM level. In practice it will exactly be the interaction between the two models which is point of departure and act as guide for the strategic and consequently the practical choices which any business must take regarding their strategic positions. However, there are other potential viewpoints and consequently other potential models.

6.5 Practical Consequences for Managers – Viewpoints and Strategy

Having established the foundation of the theory in order to "Where to Look" we conclude that a business has many potential viewpoints for "Where to

Look". The importance of the transparency of knowing the viewpoint becomes even more clear when we link to strategy. Strategy has to do with execution of the work done in the mapping, seeing and sensing phases. In the picture beneath nine different positions are demonstrated. While the positions 1, 2 and 3 have directly reference to BM CUBE level, the positions 4 and 5 have directly reference to the business level. The positions 6-9 are where the idea of eco-systems come into play – either we a talking about eco-systems from a business level point of view, a BM-Eco System from a BM-Cube level point of view or we are talking about an "Eco-system-Eco-system" and a "BM Eco-system-BM Eco-system" level point of view.

From a practical manager perspective we suggest that any manager with a responsibility at business level must involve different perspectives. Such

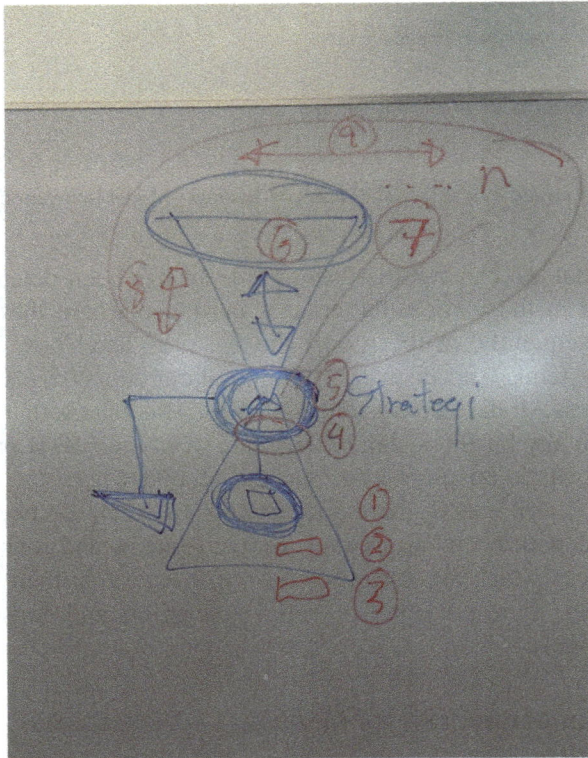

Figure 17   From a Supervision Session at Cand.Polyt, Aarhus University.

Source: Horn Rasmussen, Ole (2015), From a Supervision Session at Cand. Polyt, Aarhus University.

practice secures that the business in their strategic work creates an overview regarding their business. And most of all such practice secures that the business choses a portfolio of BMs which "work together" seen from the business perspective. There may exist situation where the business wants the BMs at CUBE-level to "compete" against each other. However, the point is that with the explicit and transparent use of the different perspective in the daily work the latter situation only occurs if wanted. We have in our practical work with the industry experienced that many businesses in fact operates – without knowing it – with competing BMs which in the long end can "kill the whole business from the inside" or – as a more decent situation – be counter productive in order to exploit the BMI potential of the business.

Another practical consequence is that managers must be aware that they have a fundamental choice when starting using the framework. It can make sense to start with a small unit within the business as the point of departure for the mapping, seeing and sensing BMI process. However, making that choice the business level and the portfolio level are by definition pushed out in the eco-system or the BM Eco-system. This is not a problem if the responsible managers are fully aware of it. This means that there is transparency about what is going on. However, many businesses want to start at a business level. Having implemented some of these steps next issue could be to do it the other way around based upon a more delimited analysis of the concrete needs.

In our analysis we end up with making a further link to strategy and what is going on, when the "Where to look models" become dynamic. In Figures 18 and 19 the situation is illustrated.

Exactly what is going on when the BMs starts "working" we as a keyword use "The idea of Strategy". In the above model focus or viewpoint is the BM-Cube level. Here the theory is that we have two distinct different activities lead by a chosen strategy.

1. Arch activity one – going on within the BM
2. Arch activity two – going on between BMs

Our hard core assumption – in the Lakatos sense – is that we have five different processes which must be implemented in order for the BM to survive. This is illustrated in the model beneath.

Many BM researchers touch upon the idea of value creation during e.g. creation and capturing. Zott et. al. (Zott, Amit & Massa 2011) have most of all focus on the idea of how value is created and captured. They write e.g. ""4) business models seek to explain how value is created and captured" (p. 2). However, they also involves the idea of delivering: "Recent advances in

Business Model Eco-systems Platforms 1, 2   3   4   5 .... n

None Relations to Business Model Level

Resting Relations to Business Model Level

Active Relations to Business Model Level

Business Model Level

Cube Dimension Level

Dimension Component Level

Dimension Sub-Component Level

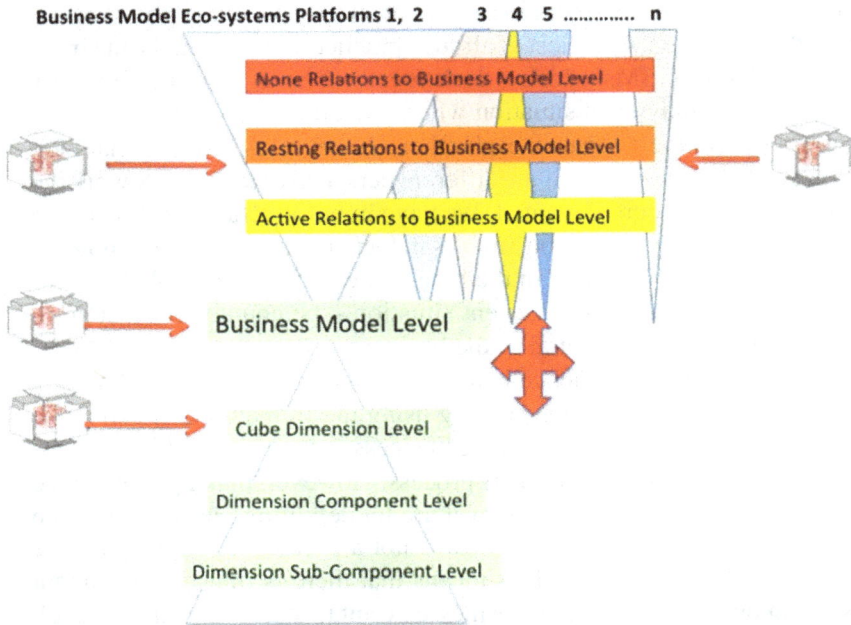

Figure 18   What is going on?

communication and information technologies, such as the emergence and swift expansion of the Internet and the rapid decline in computing and communication costs, have allowed the development of new ways to create and deliver value, which have offered scope for the creation of unconventional exchange mechanisms and transaction architectures (p. 9). And with reference to Johnson et.al. 2008) focus now is on creation and delivering: "Business models "consist of four interlocking elements, that, taken together, create and deliver value" (p. 52). These are: customer value proposition, profit formula, key resources, and key processes. (Zott, Amit & Massa 2011) These positions indicate that there are some confusion among theoreticians regarding the idea of value creation and BMs.

However, we find that there are five arch processes involved.

1. Something must be created
2. This something must be captured
3. And delivered
4. Then it must be received
5. And finally it must be consumed

Business Model Eco-systems Platforms 1, 2   3   4   5 .... n

None Relations to Business Model Level

Resting Relations to Business Model Level

Active Relations to Business Model Level

Business Model Level

Define and implement creation, capturing, delivering, receiving and consumption of values during relations in the single BM in question

Cube Dimension Level

Dimension Component Level

Dimension Sub-Component Level

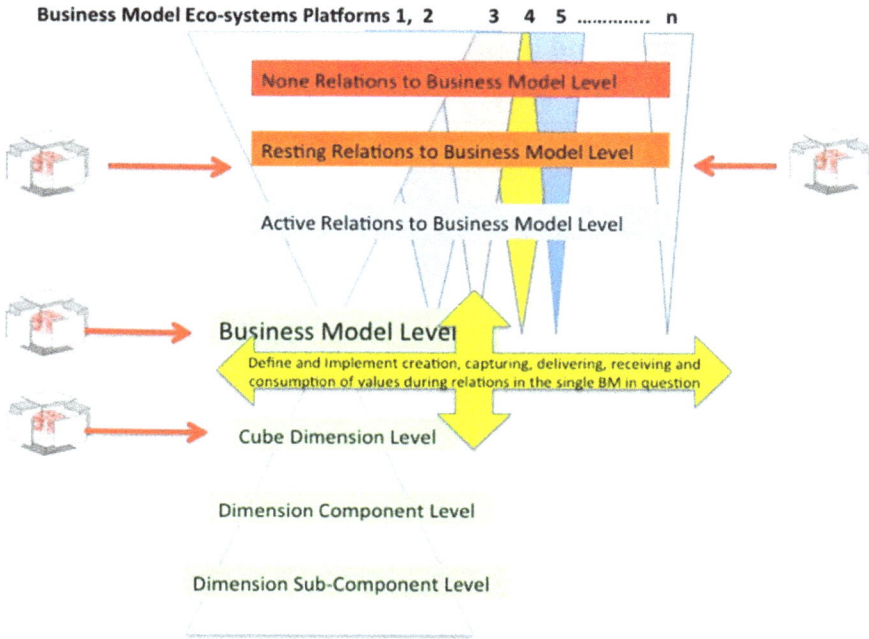

Figure 19   The Elements in the Real BM Business Model Innovation Strategy Process.

Taken the above models as a whole this means that we have the following situation where the idea of strategy is involved.

This leaves managers with the necessity to have a quite well established overview regarding their BMs. Besides it leaves managers to incorporate totally new procedures compared with the established procedures. Because how shall we define the idea of: Create, Capture, Deliver, Receive and Consume? However, this is not part of this paper.

6.6 BMES and BMI – Practical Illustration

The models evolved above can also be illustrated from at concrete BMI modeling process implemented during 3 days by a gr oup of students from Department of Business Development and Technology, Aarhus University, Denmark. 12 groups of students each with 5 members, were May, 2015, challenges to reflect over and solve a concrete challenge made by the industry and researchers at the university. One group had a challenge put up by Danish Technological Institute and Foulum, Aarhus University. The challenge was

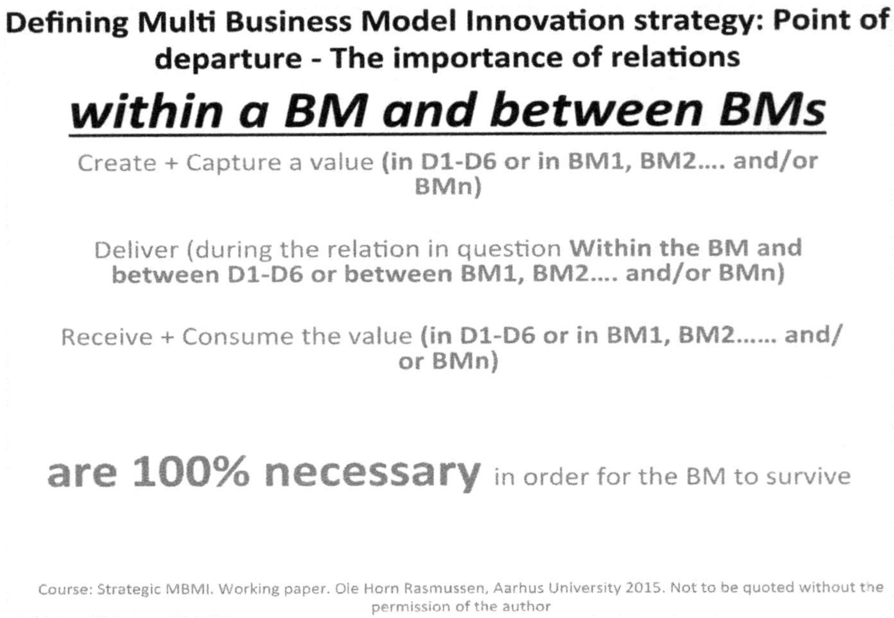

Defining Multi Business Model Innovation strategy: Point of departure - The importance of relations

within a BM and between BMs

Create + Capture a value **(in D1-D6 or in BM1, BM2…. and/or BMn)**

Deliver (during the relation in question **Within the BM and between D1-D6 or between BM1, BM2…. and/or BMn)**

Receive + Consume the value **(in D1-D6 or in BM1, BM2…… and/ or BMn)**

are 100% necessary in order for the BM to survive

Course: Strategic MBMI. Working paper. Ole Horn Rasmussen, Aarhus University 2015. Not to be quoted without the permission of the author

Figure 20   Toward a Definition of Multi Business Model Innovation strategy. Course Slide, 2015.

Source: Horn Rasmussen, Ole (2015), Strategic MBMI. Working Paper for Master Course, Aarhus University.

a question of how to organize a new kind of food production based upon insects. This group mapped the current situation "AS-IS" and based upon the current situation they proposed an entirely new eco-system, which were organized across existing eco-systems who only partly were connected. The TO-BE business model were in fact evolved as a combination of a lot of existing BMs, however organized in another way and with another purpose. The reason why the students could create a new BM eco-system was their ability modeling upon eco-systems which today are connected together with eco-systems which never had been connected before. Besides, their idea is a sustainable BMES which so to speak "feed itself" during recirculation. The value formula are consistent during different tools which secure that each relation create value and the way the BMES could exist was secured by putting the consultant company LARLA in the core of the BMES. They implement what we pronounce "BMES Strategic Leadership". Compared with "real life" they created a position for LARLA which can be compared with an "BMES

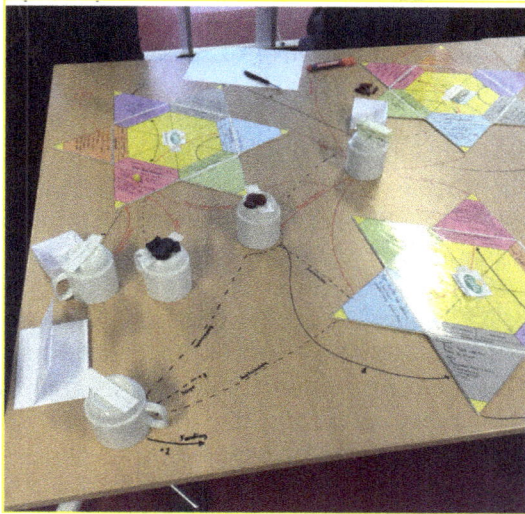

Figure 21 Students working with practical BMI Challenges at Cand. Polyt, Aarhus University, 2015.

Strategic Leadership" position created and implemented by e.g. Google and Apple. Or within an Veblenian theoretical context they are in a position as "The Captain of Industry".

6.7 Summing Up

Today, most academia's and practitioners consider the BM as a part of a market, an industry, sector or a cluster. Although there are many different definitions and types of business groups most define these related to a businessmodel at a business level. However, as demonstrated there is a need for a distinction between levels of business model focus. The fundamental reason is that any business consists of more than one business model within our framework. If one solely choose a business level focus the data focus will become fluffy because different business models is mixed. To obtain a solid BMI knowledge base with a focus on the specific BMs AS-IS position it is necessary to "step down" from a business level focus to a BM level focus. Turning the attention to eco-system level we have underlined a need for a model, where the BM in question refers to BMES, which is a more specific reference compared with the idea of eco-systems. We further propose that the BMES level should have focus in research as "forming" an "umbrella" of "AS IS" and "TO

BE" BM's represented in a specific BMES. As indicated we transfer our understanding of the relation-axiom at the BM-level to the BMES level. This means that the BMI process at BMES level not only pays attention on related BMES's but also pay attention to BMES that are not related. This is to prevent fuzziness and support discussions for further development of a firm BM theory. The BMES vertical and horizontal level is considered as being complex and the BMES diversification is maybe the most complex level of BMES BMI. This may be the reason why it is often not used by BMES to secure their survival. However, understanding a BMES as a Cube can be useful for creation of AS-IS and TO-BE BMES-data. Data for "on the way to begin operating" ("TO BE" BMES's) and on BMESs "already operating" ("AS IS" BMES's). Even the abstraction at this point is high we don't find any arguments that can counteract the relevance of the above statements and the above way of logic. In this manner we have arguments to include the above thinking into the theoretical "hard core" in the Lakatos sense and consequently we have some elements which contribute to a theory of BM and BMI.

There are until now not an accepted language developed for BMES's nor is the term BMES generally accepted in the Business Model Literature. The research show that the old thinking of industry, sector and cluster systems defined these days are challenged because it gives the business and the industry a kind of false security related to what is really the market, industry, sector or cluster. Especially when competitors or other businesses and BMES begin to define the BMES different – context based – then "conservative" thinking businesses and industries are challenges. The need for strategy and competitive tools is inherent because many businesses have formulated their strategy on behalf of market, industry, sector and cluster thinking.

As a supplement and opposite to market, industry, sector and cluster definitions we propose a different terminology – the Business Model Cube and Business Model Ecosystem (BMES) defined as related to a context based approach and including both "AS IS" and "TO BE" BM's. We propose that any BMES can be defined related to 7 dimensions (value proposition, user and customers, value chain function, competence, network, value formula and relations). The BM is the focus as the smallest part of any BMES opposite to previous terms using the business as the focus.

Having established a position for "Where to Look" the next issue is the question "How to Look"? Which methods? and How to do this? This is not part of this paper. We have been going from theory with a few empirical illustration in order to identify potential links which makes sense. Such methodology doesn't verify any theory. However, the indications tell us that we have some results which give meaning for the search for a research program in the Lakatos sense. We are aware of that our verifying focussed methodology must go close in hand with the proposed ontology and we are aware of a need to try to "shoot our hypothesis down". However, this is not part of the mission in this paper.

7 Conclusion

This paper is conceptual and aims to contribute to the ontological, episte-mological and methodological discussion toward a theory of business model and business model innovation. Focus is a contribution for a definition of the object for where a business must look in order to optimize their investment in innovation processes. In the Lakatos sense the paper aims to contribute to the establishment of a research program for business model innovation on the one side and on the other side the paper aims to support the practical BMI efforts to implement concrete BMI actions in the businesses.

Before a business is able to implement a well qualified work for "How to Look?" and "How to implement" BMI it is important for a business to know "Where to look?" The paper contributes by qualifying with an answer to "Where must managers look in order to release the BMI potential of their business?" during deepening the understanding of the two black boxes – a business and the surrounding of the business – and the coherence between them. The paper aims to argue that we simply cannot take the two black boxes for given and demonstrates how a combined top-down and bottom-up perspective opens up for different new models for "Where to look".

Trying to have a holistic approach we are forced to investigate if and how different approaches are able to work together. What we ask for is a need to establish a holistic approach in order to optimize the business model innovation work in a business. We must establish an overview that reflects the whole "battlefield" for a business. Our hypothesis for a contribution to a solution is to combine different perspectives of abstraction and then link these perspectives to the idea of a business and how a business is organized into a number of different business models operating in what we call the relation-axiom of business models. The hypothesis is that the relation-axiom of business models assists us in getting an overview of the business. By combining an inside-out, an outside-in, an inside-in and an outside-out perspective during the relation axiom we offer a new BMI tool for both the academic theoretical work and the practical work in any business – public, private, organization, departments, a separate unit within a business etc. The BMI tool contributes to create an overview. This is crucial before any attempts to do BMI strategically are taken by the business. Explain and understand BMI and the process of BMI may profit by integration of different perspectives of the economic system because taken together the perspectives reflect the framework conditions for the implementation of BMI.

Summed up we have pointed on:

1. The idea of national systems of innovation must be supplemented with other perspective. The hypothesis is that the idea of a national system of innovation is too narrow in order to explain and understand the economic process of BMI.
2. The idea of clusters, sectors and industries is based upon the understanding of a business as the unit in focus. This idea of thinking must be supplemented with other perspectives because any business – by definition – consists of more than one BM.
3. The BM focus creates a need for supplement the "old" single business model focus with a "new" multi business model focus.
4. Within a multi business model focus the coherence and interplay between AS-IS BM and TO BE BM represents a theoretical and practical necessity in order to understand the economic organization and the dynamic economic organization at micro as well as macro economic level.
5. The idea of "Stick to your core business" and "Focus on your core competences" represents within the new theoretically multi BM understanding a risky strategy for any business who implement such strategy.
6. It might be valuable to rethink the term entry- and exit barriers to and borders to industry, clusters and sectors – and instead think them as context based. The borders of ecosystems and BMES depends on the context and the viewpoint.
7. The idea of "Context borders" might give us different and even better strategic advantage to previous terms.
8. Concrete experiences with BM construction – or in our framework BMI – point on the importance of a focus on different sub-areas and the idea of co-option. Besides experiences point at the need to incorporate the idea of time and the different velocity or clock-speed that the different sub-systems represents. All this influence if or if not the innovation becomes a successful or an un-successful innovation.
9. The idea of a global system of eco-systems seems to enrich the discussion of framework conditions for the BMI process. A main point is that a

concrete and practical focus on eco-systems also puts focus on the "unborn" business opportunities – or what we in our framework terms: TO-BE Business Model.

10. Point of departure and a contribution could as a hypothesis be, that the idea of a business must be defined differently, where the idea of a business consisting of a number of different business models representing the portfolio of the business' "AS-IS" and "To-Be" business models seems adequate as a starting point.

11. The idea of a business-model as a cube has in our paticipative action research approach worked in practice. However, the idea of the need to break down the business not only into different business models but to break down each business model into different dimensions and further into different components seems interesting, and the hypothesis is that it enriches the explanation and understanding of the actual releasing of the innovation potential in the BMI process.

12. Based upon the idea of eco-systems and the idea that any business consists of more than one BM make it necessary to introduce and work with the idea of BMESs.

13. The Veblenian general theory – which put the evolutionary economic business process into an institutional and actor teleological context – contributes to enrich explanation and understanding of the economic process including the BMI process and BMES. We have indications that The Veblenian General Theory enriches the explanatory power and understanding of the BMI framework condition at a micro level within specific fragments. The Better Place case illustrated that the question of "Where to look?" when a business implement BMI can be qualified by involving a pure theoretical Veblenian thinking and transfer the theoretical thinking into an empiric business case or object.

In the paper we presented what we as a hypothesis see as the research field for any business working and implementing business model innovation. The idea of defining and understand a research field at a general level of abstraction is the first demand to the business. We now have offered a contribution for "Where to Look?". When we talk about a general level of abstraction it is important to underline, that the empirical feed-back up to now has been fragmentary. However, exactly this abstract world becomes concrete when any business goes through a BMI process. Any BM is unique. The consequence will be that every business will have its own, specific and context dependent research field or what we have termed Business Model Eco-Systems (BMESs). Of course different businesses will have a research field, which at first glance seems identical. However, our hypothesis is that such situation is by definition never existing, because any business model is unique. The uniqueness of the BM will be clearly demonstrated when the concrete mapping process in form of the downloading phase and the seeing phase of the BM in question has been implemented. Having established a contribution to a framework for "Where to Look?" next step will be to contribute to the question of "How to Look?".

Appendix I (Source: (Horn Rasmussen 2008, page 87))

Mechanism 1: "Interstitial Adjustments"

Veblen introduces the concept of "The Interstitial Adjustments of the Industrial System". We interpret it as a fundamental mechanism in his theory. *Interstitial adjustment characterises the inherent mechanism of the aims of different groups of businessmen to create or hinder the instability of the industrial system*[12]. The point of departure is the inherent contradiction between the interest of the community as a whole and the businessmen. "Instability" is of great importance to certain groups of businessmen because of the possibility to realise large gains. "The end is pecuniary gain, the mean is disturbances of the industrial system" (Veblen 1904: 16)[13]. Especially the new and rising class of pecuniary experts "whose business is strategic management of the interstitial relations of the system" (Veblen 1904: 17) is claimed to have interest in large disturbances. This class is "the captains", and their operations must be understood with reference to obtaining control over some large portion of the industrial system. When the control is obtained, the interest of the captains is to maintain business conditions as they are and to further facilitate the support of the position. The position of the businessmen shifts from an interest in instability to a wish for continuity. Anything in their interest relates

---

[12]The concepts of "sabotage" and "waste" play a major role in the process of interstitial adjustment. The "interstitial adjustment" mechanism is present at any time, as are "sabotage" and "waste". However, dealing with these concepts has been chosen to be part of the "Institution Competitive System". We could have categorised both concepts as part of the "interstitial adjustment" mechanism, but we find that "sabotage" and "waste" contain so many dynamic- and context-dependent elements that we would lose some of the dynamics pointed out by Veblen in doing so.

[13]In order to understand the mechanism, it must be noted that Veblen does not include the so-called "old-fashioned businessmen" in this group of businessmen. The old-fashioned businessmen are those using "the old-fashioned method of permanent investment in some one industrial or commercial plan" (Veblen 1904: 16).

to the ability to obtain gains. Their aim is pecuniary optimising. The method is to use transactions and make deals ("the business jargon borrowed from gaming slang" (Veblen 1904: 18)).

References

[1] Abell, D.F. 1980, *Defining the business: the starting point of strategic planning*, Prentice-Hall Englewood Cliffs, NJ.

[2] Afuah, A. 2003, "Redefining firm boundaries in the face of the internet: are firms really shrinking?", *Academy of Management Review*, vol. 28, no. 1, pp. 34–53.

[3] Amit, R. & Zott, C. 2012, "Creating Value Through Business Model Innovation", *MIT Sloan Management Review*, vol. 53, no. 3, pp. 41–49.

[4] Casadesus-Masanell, R. & Ricart, J.E. 2010a, "From strategy to business models and onto tactics", *Long range planning*, vol. 43, no. 2, pp. 195–215.

[5] Casadesus-Masanell, R. & Ricart, J.E. 2010b, "From strategy to business models and onto tactics", *Long range planning*, vol. 43, no. 2, pp. 195–215.

[6] Chesbrough, H.W. 2007, *Open business models: how to thrive in the new innovation landscape*, Harvard Business School, Boston, Mass.

[7] Costanza, R., Cumberland, J., Daly, H., Goodland, R., Norgaard, R. & International Society for Ecological Economics, Washington, DC (EUA) 1997, "An introduction to ecological economics."

[8] DeLong, J. 2000, "Why the valley way is here to stay", *Fortune*, vol. 141, no. 11, pp. 36–37.

[9] Dougherty, D. 1992, "Interpretive barriers to successful product innovation in large firms", *Organization Science*, vol. 3, no. 2, pp. 179–202.

[10] Elster, J. 1983, *Explaining technical change*, Universitetsforlaget, Oslo.

[11] Freeman, C. 1995, "The 'National System of Innovation' in historical perspective", *Cambridge Journal of economics*, vol. 19, no. 1, pp. 5–24.

[12] Grønkjær, L. 2015, *tiel mangler*.

[13] Heikkilä, M. & Kuivaniemi, L. 2012, "Ecosystem under construction: an action research study on entrepreneurship in a business ecosystem", *Technology Innovation Management Review*, vol. 2, no. 6.

[14] Horn Rasmussen, O. & Lindgren, P. 2013, *Workshop photo Vertical Butterfly, October 2013*.

[15] Horn Rasmussen, O. 2008, *Evolution of Organic Agriculture within Theoretical Frameworks of Structural Change and Transformation*, Aalborg University.

[16] Horn Rasmussen, O. 2013, *E-mail corspondence*.

[17] Horn Rasmussen, O. 2013 (January), *The first version of The vertical Butterfly*.

[18] Horn Rasmussen, O., 2015, From a Supervision Session at Cand. Polyt, Aarhus University.

[19] Horn Rasmussen, O., Lindgren, P. & Saghaug, K.F. 2014, "Business model Eco systems and Intellectual Capital II: Why is Intellectual Capital from business BM's relations not released from a general Veblenian framework condition perspective?", vol. IFKAD, 2014 Conference Paper, Zagreb.

[20] Horn Rasmussen, Ole (2015), Strategic MBMI. Working Paper for Master Course, Aarhus University.

[21] http://en.wikipedia.org/wiki/National System of Innovation, March, 2013.

[22] Kotler, P. & Armstrong, G. 2010, *Principles of marketing*, Pearson Education.

[23] Kotler, P. 1983, *Principles of Marketing*.

[24] Langager, C. 2015, *What is the difference between an industry and a sector?*. Available: http://www.investopedia.com/ask/answers/05/industrysector.asp [2015, June].

[25] Latsis, S.J. (ed) 1976, *Methods and Appraisal in Economics*, Cambridge University Press, Cambridge.

[26] Lawson, T. 1997, *Economics and reality*, Routledge, London.

[27] Lawson, T. 2003a, "Institutionalism: on the need to firm up notions of social structure and the human subject", *Journal of Economic Issues*, pp. 175–207.

[28] Lawson, T. 2003b, *Reorienting economics*, Psychology Press.

[29] Lazonick, W. 2010, "Innovative business models and varieties of capitalism: Financialization of the US corporation", *Business History Review*, vol. 84, no. 04, pp. 675–702.

[30] Lecocq, X., Demil, B. & Ventura, J. 2010, "Business models as a research program in strategic management: an appraisal based on Lakatos", *M@ n@ gement*, vol. 13, no. 4, pp. 214–225.

[31] Lindgreen, A., Davis, R., Brodie, R.J. & Buchanan-Oliver, M. 2000, "Pluralism in contemporary marketing practices", *International Journal of Bank Marketing*, vol. 18, no. 6, pp. 294–308.

[32] Lindgren, P. & Horn Rasmussen, O. 2013, "The business model cube", *Journal of Multi Business Model Innovation and Technology*, vol. 1, no. 2, pp. 135–182.

[33] Lindgren, P., Taran, Y. & Boer, H. 2010, "From single firm to network-based business model innovation", *International Journal of Entrepreneurship and Innovation Management*, vol. 12, no. 2, pp. 122–137.

[34] Lundvall, B. 2010, *National systems of innovation: Toward a theory of innovation and interactive learning*, Anthem Press.

[35] Magretta, J. 2002, "Why business models matter".

[36] Markides, C.C. 2013, "Business model innovation: What can the ambidexterity literature teach us?", *The Academy of Management Perspectives*, vol. 27, no. 4, pp. 313–323.

[37] Moore, J.F. 1993, "Predators and prey: a new ecology of competition", *Harvard business review*, vol. 71, no. 3, pp. 75–83.

[38] Moore, J.F. 1996, *The death of competition: leadership and strategy in the age of business ecosystems*, HarperBusiness New York.

[39] Moore, J.F. 1998, "The rise of a new corporate form", *Washington Quarterly*, vol. 21, no. 1, pp. 167–181.

[40] Moore, J.F. 2006, "Business ecosystems and the view from the firm", *Antitrust Bull.*, vol. 51, pp. 31.

[41] Morris, M., Schindehutte, M. & Allen, J. 2005, "The entrepreneur's business model: toward a unified perspective", *Journal of business research*, vol. 58, no. 6, pp. 726–735.

[42] Nelson, R.R. 1993, "National innovation systems: a comparative analysis", *University of Illinois at Urbana-Champaign's Academy for Entrepreneurial Leadership Historical Research Reference in Entrepreneurship*.

[43] Nelson, R. (ed.) (1993), "National Innovation Systems. A Comparative Analysis, Oxford University Press, New York/Oxford". http://en.wikipedia.org/wiki/National System of Innovation (March, 2013).

[44] Norgaard, R.B. 1994, "Development betrayed. The end of a progress and a co-evolutionary revision of the future", no. London and New York, Routledge.

[45] Osterwalder, A., Pigneur, Y. & Tucci, C.L. 2005, "Clarifying business models: Origins, present, and future of the concept", *Communications of the association for Information Systems*, vol. 16, no. 1, pp. 1.

[46] Porter, M.E. 1985, "Competitive advantage: creating and sustaining competitive performance", *Competitive advantage: creating and sustaining competitive performance*.

[47] Porter, M.E. 1998, *Clusters and the new economics of competition*, Harvard Business Review Boston.

[48] Prahalad, C. & Hamel, G. 1990, "The core competence of the corporation", *Boston (Ma)*, vol. 1990, pp. 235–256.

[49] Schumpeter, J.A. 1983 (1934), *The theory of economic development: An inquiry into profits, capital, credit, interest, and the business cycle*, Transaction publishers.

[50] Shuen, A., Feiler, P.F. & Teece, D.J. 2014, "Dynamic capabilities in the upstream oil and gas sector: Managing next generation competition", *Energy Strategy Reviews*.

[51] Teece, D.J. 2010, "Business models, business strategy and innovation", *Long range planning*, vol. 43, no. 2, pp. 172–194.

[52] Teece, D.J. 2014, "A dynamic capabilities-based entrepreneurial theory of the multinational enterprise", *Journal of International Business Studies*, vol. 45, no. 1, pp. 8–37.

[53] Teece, D.J. 2015, "Chapter 16 – Technological Innovation and the Theory of the Firm: The Role of Enterprise-Level Knowledge, Complementarities, and (Dynamic) Capabilities" in *Handbook of the Economics of Innovation* North-Holland, pp. 679–730.

[54] Veblen, T. 1914, *The Instinct of Workmanship: And the State of Industrial Arts*, Macmillan.

[55] Veblen, T. 1978, *The theory of business enterprise*, Transaction Publishers.

[56] Zott, C. & Amit, R. 2013, "The business model: A theoretically anchored robust construct for strategic analysis", *Strategic Organization*, vol. 11, no. 4, pp. 403.

[57] Zott, C., Amit, R. & Massa, L. 2011, "The business model: recent developments and future research", *Journal of management*, vol. 37, no. 4, pp. 1019–1042.

Biographies

O. Horn Rasmussen is Postdoc at Aarhus University. He holds a M.Sc. in Economics and a Ph.D. in Evolution of Technological Systems within Theoretical Frameworks of Structural Change and Transformation. His research interests are within the scientific field multi business model innovation, co-existence of old and new technologies, economics and the economic process. Before commitment to Aarhus University he was Post-Doctoral Fellow at the Department of Mechanical and Manufacturing Engineering, Aalborg University, Denmark. He has been Ph.D and Researcher at the Department of Economics, Politics and Public Administration and Department of Business and Economics at Aalborg University. His research interest ranges from (i) Business Model Innovation (ii) Strategic Business Model Innovation, Scenario Modeling, Business Accelerator and Sustainability (iii) Business Model Ecosystems (iv) Business Models, Engineering, Interdisciplinarity and Research Ontology, Epistemology and Methodology (v) Economics and the Economic Process. His empiric research methodology is a paticipative action research approach. The aim is to innovate new models and methods for integrated technology and business model innovation across product, service, production and process technology platforms in mind bothering multiple spin-outs. He works across industries, companies, public and private in order to create radically new solutions and integrable knowledge of those involved partners. To master the total integrated technology and business model innovation process from idea, concept, prototype implementation to operation, commercialization and bottom line is a prime goal. The results are incorporated into university educational programs, courses and training modules for students and Ph.D Schools.

P. Lindgren is Full Professor of Multi Business Innovation and Technology at Aarhus University, Denmark. He holds B.Sc in Business Administration, M.Sc in Foreign Trade and Ph.D. in Network-based High Speed Innovation. He has (co-)authored numerous articles and several books on subjects such as product development in metwork, electronic product development, new global business development, innovation management and leadership, and high speed innovation. His current research interest is in new global business models, i.e. the typology and generic types of business models and how to innovate them.

Author Index

Keywords Index

B

Business Management 62
Business Model Eco-Systems 60,
    62, 94, 107
Business Model Theory
    Construction 62
Business network 29, 30, 32, 39
Business value 1, 13, 15, 18
Business model 2, 8, 31, 41
Business Theory 62

C

Co-creation 29, 30, 41, 46
Collaboration 7, 29, 46
Coordination 29, 30, 34, 48, 78

E

Economic Theory 62
Eco-Systems 60, 65, 67, 94
Empirical Object 62, 63

F

Fairness 29, 30, 32, 45
Framework Conditions for Business
    Model Innovation 62

Function 1, 3, 6, 12
Functional Product 1, 2, 20, 23
Functional Sales 1, 6

I

Industrial Product-Service
    System 1, 2, 6
Innovation model 1, 3, 12, 18
Innovation 1, 4, 8, 18

L

Lakatos 59, 62, 65, 115
Learning 10, 29, 33, 46

M

Manufacturing industry 1, 6, 13
Methodology 4, 61, 74

P

Product-Service System 1, 6, 21

S

Sustainability 1, 9, 13, 123

www.ingramcontent.com/pod-product-compliance
Lightning Source LLC
Chambersburg PA
CBHW061839220326
41599CB00027B/5345